The
SCORPIO
Path

YOUR DAILY 2026 HOROSCOPE GUIDE

AMANDA M CLARKE

Copyright © Amanda M Clarke 2026
KORU Publishing

All rights reserved. All content, materials, and intellectual property in this book or any other platform owned by Koru Publishing are protected by copyright laws. This includes text, images, graphics, videos, audio, software, and any other form of content that may be produced by Koru Publishing.

No part of this content may be reproduced, distributed, or transmitted in any form or by any means without the prior written permission of Koru Publishing. This means that you cannot copy, reproduce, or use any of the content in this book for commercial or personal purposes without the express written consent of Koru Publishing.

Unauthorized use of any copyrighted material owned by Koru Publishing may result in legal action being taken against you. Koru Publishing reserves the right to pursue all available legal remedies against any individual or entity found to be infringing on its copyright.

In summary, Koru Publishing © 2024 holds exclusive rights to all the content produced by it, and any unauthorized use of such content will result in legal action.

KORU Publishing

KORU (Maori:NZ)
A symbol of spiritual growth and spiritual connection.

Rocky Point Townhouse, CHRISTMAS ISLAND, Western Australia 6798

ISBN: 978-1-923614-08-6

More on the Bookshelves at
www.theliteraryoracle.com

Disclaimer: The Scorpio Path: Your daily 2026 horoscope guide book provides information on astrological readings and intuitive interpretations, it is not intended as a substitute for professional advice, diagnosis, or treatment. The information contained in this book is provided for educational and entertainment purposes only and is not meant to be taken as specific advice for individual circumstances. The author and publisher make no representations or warranties with respect to the accuracy or completeness of the contents of this book and specifically disclaim any implied warranties of merchantability or fitness for a particular purpose. The reader should always consult with a licensed professional for any specific concerns or questions. The author and publisher shall not be liable for any loss or damage caused or alleged to have been caused, directly or indirectly, by the information contained in this book. The use of this book is at the reader's sole risk

More from Amanda Clarke
The Literary Oracle
www.theliteracyoracle.com

The "Daily Guidance" series offers an innovative approach to finding spiritual wisdom and practical advice. Each book in the series is a unique tool designed for daily introspection and decision-making. Readers are invited to meditate on a question or seek general guidance for the day, then flip to a random page in the book. The page they land on provides a personalized message from various spiritual sources, such as angels, tarot, or spirit animals. With each turn of the page, these books deliver insightful, positive messages and mantras to inspire personal growth and provide clarity on life's daily challenges and decisions.

Other books in this series:-
The Angelic Oracles
Daily Angel Tarot Reading
Mystic Tarot Cat
Oracle of the Tarot Cat
Vibes Unveiled
Spirit Animal Oracle
Answers from the Oracles
Messages from the Angels

Daily Guidance
SERIES

Supporting Indie Authors

Love your daily guidance? You can grab more of my books direct from The Literary Oracle:
www.theliteraryoracle.com

Buying direct means:
- Much better prices for you + free shipping.
- More support for me as an indie author
- More magical books in your hands

My books are also available worldwide through online bookstores, but direct purchases help keep the magic flowing.

Thank you for supporting indie creativity!

Scan me

Welcome to The Scorpio Path: Your Daily 2026 Horoscope Guide — your deeply intuitive, transformative companion for the year ahead. Crafted for the powerful, passionate, and resilient Scorpio, this guide honours the way you move through life — with emotional depth, unwavering focus, and an inner strength that thrives in both shadows and light.

Inside, you'll find daily horoscopes paired with affirmations designed to align with your natural intensity and insight. Each reading is here to help you embrace 2026 with courage, whether you're pursuing ambitious goals, strengthening relationships, prioritising your well-being, or uncovering the hidden truths that guide your evolution.

This isn't about control — it's about transformation. As you turn each page, you'll discover clarity, encouragement, and powerful reminders from the cosmos, urging you to trust your instincts and embrace change. Let this be the year you rise fully into your power, live authentically, and step boldly into the magic of your destiny.

The Answers You Seek

Are Within

January 2026

Scorpio
01 January 2026

Scorpio, the year begins with a cosmic nudge toward clarity. The Moon illuminates your emotional depths, reminding you to release last year's clutter. The Sun in harmony with Mercury sharpens your voice—today is excellent for setting intentions, journaling, or having important conversations. If you feel torn between expectations and authenticity, lean toward honesty. This is a fresh slate—don't carry old baggage into it. Your intensity is a gift, but channel it toward growth rather than control. The stars encourage you to claim your desires unapologetically and trust they'll magnetize opportunities.

Affirmation & Gratitude

I start the year with gratitude, releasing what no longer serves me and inviting clarity, honesty, and authentic growth.

Scorpio
02 January 2026

Today, Scorpio, healing energies surround you. Old doubts may surface, but instead of resisting, see them as reminders of strength gained. Mars fuels ambition, yet Saturn whispers patience. Don't rush—what you're building needs steady foundations. A boundary may be tested; this is your moment to hold firm without guilt. Your intuition is sharp, so honor it without second-guessing. Balance is key—blend action with self-care. A walk outdoors or mindful stillness will restore your focus. Transformation begins quietly today, reminding you that power lies in persistence and inner trust, not speed.

Affirmation & Gratitude

I honor my strength by embracing patience and gratitude, trusting steady steps and intuition to guide my transformation today.

Scorpio
03 January 2026

Scorpio, today's cosmic focus falls on money and self-worth. Venus enhances your resource zone, hinting at opportunities for abundance or creative income streams. Be alert—opportunities may appear in conversations or unexpected offers. Yet Neptune can cloud details; don't rush decisions without reading the fine print. Deeper still, the stars remind you that financial choices reflect your self-value. Are you undervaluing yourself or underselling your worth? Today invites you to set standards that align with your true power. Practical yet visionary thinking will create long-lasting benefits. Trust yourself to invest wisely.

Affirmation & Gratitude

I am grateful for opportunities to expand abundance, honoring my worth and making empowered choices that secure long-term stability.

Scorpio
04 January 2026

Scorpio, mental clarity is your gift today. Mercury highlights problem-solving, so long-standing challenges may finally make sense. Your insight pierces veils others can't see through. This is a strong day for writing, planning, or speaking truth with precision. Be mindful—your words carry weight, so use them kindly. Emotional flow is steady, giving you strength to balance vulnerability with resilience. The universe may send you signs through repeating numbers or vivid dreams. Pay attention. Your inner compass is aligned, offering direction where confusion once lingered. Trust your intellect and intuition equally today.

Affirmation & Gratitude

I am grateful for clear insight and guidance, trusting my sharp mind and intuitive wisdom to navigate every challenge.

Scorpio
05 January 2026

Relationships take center stage today, Scorpio. The Sun highlights your partnership sector, asking for honesty, balance, and deeper commitment. Tensions may arise, but they're opportunities to strengthen bonds rather than weaken them. If single, you may notice magnetic attraction—follow it with curiosity, not fear. Passion is strong, but Saturn reminds you real connections grow through patience and mutual respect. A heartfelt conversation can reset dynamics for the better. Remember: being present and listening deeply creates more transformation than control ever could. This day strengthens your ties through authenticity and empathy.

Affirmation & Gratitude

I welcome balance and gratitude in my relationships, honoring love, respect, and mutual growth in every connection today.

Scorpio
06 January 2026

Scorpio, the stars light up your career and purpose. Jupiter boosts your confidence—today is ideal for stepping into leadership or sharing ideas. Recognition could come unexpectedly, so polish how you present yourself. Mars fires ambition, but Saturn advises persistence over impatience. Don't underestimate small, consistent actions; they're building your bigger future. If an opportunity arises, trust your gut to seize it. The universe pushes you to stand out with integrity, depth, and originality. Your work isn't just what you do—it's how you embody your calling with conviction.

Affirmation & Gratitude

I am grateful for courage and purpose, confidently stepping into opportunities that align with integrity and long-term success.

Scorpio
07 January 2026

Scorpio, today calls for rest and inner renewal. The Moon pulls you inward, encouraging you to slow down and reconnect with your soul. You may feel sensitive to others' moods, but instead of resisting, use it to deepen your empathy. Creativity flows if you allow space—art, music, or journaling will soothe your spirit. Neptune amplifies your dreams, offering guidance through symbolism—pay attention. This isn't a day to force progress but to gather strength for what's ahead. Trust that rest is productive; it restores your resilience and vision.

Affirmation & Gratitude

I honor the gift of rest, grateful for quiet moments that restore balance, insight, and energy for my journey ahead.

Scorpio
08 January 2026

Scorpio, today shines a spotlight on communication and connections. Mercury enhances your ability to speak clearly, while Venus softens your words, making them more persuasive. This is a day to reach out, network, or resolve lingering misunderstandings. If you've been holding back your truth, the stars encourage expression without fear. Your words can open doors and heal divides. Pay attention to written agreements too—details matter now. The energy supports learning, writing, or teaching. Inspiration may strike suddenly, reminding you that your voice has value, power, and reach. Use it wisely.

Affirmation & Gratitude

I am grateful for my voice, using words with clarity and kindness to build connections and inspire positive change.

Scorpio
09 January 2026

Today, Scorpio, the focus turns toward your home and emotional foundations. The Moon calls you inward to nurture your sanctuary. Family matters may arise, giving you a chance to resolve tension or strengthen bonds. It's also a day to ground yourself by creating order in your environment—declutter, rearrange, or simply light a candle to invite peace. You thrive when your base feels secure, so prioritize comfort today. Listen to your inner child; what does it need right now? When your roots feel strong, your branches can reach higher.

Affirmation & Gratitude

I honor my need for grounding, grateful for a safe and nurturing space that restores my strength and peace today.

Scorpio
10 January 2026

Scorpio, creative energy surges today, urging you to express yourself boldly. Whether through art, writing, or heartfelt conversation, your passion shines. Romantic energy also intensifies—flirtation or deepening intimacy feels natural now. The cosmos encourages joy and playfulness, reminding you life isn't only about transformation and responsibility. Lean into hobbies or activities that reignite your spark. Children or youthful energy may also inspire you to reconnect with fun. Don't dismiss lightheartedness as unimportant—it feeds your soul. Today, expression is your medicine, and joy is your power. Allow yourself to shine unapologetically.

Affirmation & Gratitude

I embrace gratitude for joy, expressing my creativity and passion freely, and welcoming love and inspiration into my life.

Scorpio
11 January 2026

Scorpio, today highlights health and daily routines. If your energy has felt scattered, the cosmos now urges you to find balance. Evaluate your habits—are they supporting or draining you? Small adjustments can make huge differences. Focus on hydration, nourishment, and mindful movement. Work matters may also require discipline—your ability to cut through distractions is strong, so use it to tackle tasks efficiently. Remember, service to others is noble, but not at the cost of your own wellbeing. Balance responsibility with self-care, and you'll emerge stronger, sharper, and revitalized.

Affirmation & Gratitude

I am grateful for health and balance, choosing habits that support vitality, clarity, and strength in all areas of my life.

Scorpio
12 January 2026

Scorpio, partnership energy intensifies today, bringing focus to how you share yourself with others. The cosmos may stir emotions—conflicts can surface, but they're mirrors showing where balance is missing. Use this as a chance to deepen honesty, whether with a partner, friend, or colleague. For singles, attraction could feel magnetic, but take time to explore it slowly. Mars fuels passion, yet Saturn insists on responsibility—so prioritize integrity over impulse. Powerful transformation in relationships is possible now if you embrace both vulnerability and accountability. True connection requires courage, and you have it.

Affirmation & Gratitude

I am grateful for meaningful connections, embracing honesty, balance, and respect in all relationships that nurture my growth and love.

Scorpio
13 January 2026

Scorpio, your career and reputation come into sharp focus today. Opportunities for advancement may present themselves, but only if you step forward with confidence. A leader or authority figure could notice your dedication—stay prepared. The cosmos pushes you to show your capability without arrogance. Balance ambition with humility, and your authenticity will shine. If you've been doubting your path, clarity begins to emerge. Remember, your career isn't just about status—it's about aligning with purpose. Own your power, but also own your responsibility to use it wisely.

Affirmation & Gratitude

I give thanks for career opportunities, embracing confidence, authenticity, and purpose as I take bold yet grounded steps forward.

Scorpio
14 January 2026

Scorpio, the stars invite you to pause and replenish today. Your energy may dip, signaling the need for rest and reflection. This isn't failure; it's wisdom. The Moon amplifies intuition, making quiet moments rich with guidance. Meditation, journaling, or simply being still will reveal answers. Pay attention to your dreams or inner nudges—they're not random but messages guiding your next steps. Don't underestimate the power of restoration. By listening inward, you prepare yourself for greater breakthroughs ahead. Rest is not retreat—it's preparation for renewal.

Affirmation & Gratitude

I honor gratitude in stillness, trusting rest and reflection to restore my energy and reveal the wisdom I need.

Scorpio
15 January 2026

Scorpio, today the cosmos stirs your social life. Friendships, networks, and groups come into focus. You may feel drawn toward like-minded people who inspire your growth. Collaboration brings opportunity, but be mindful of those who drain your energy. A conversation with a friend could spark an idea worth pursuing. The stars also remind you that your vision expands when shared—don't isolate yourself. Connections you nurture now may open doors later in the year. Balance loyalty with discernment, and you'll know exactly where to invest your presence and passion.

Affirmation & Gratitude

I am grateful for supportive friendships and meaningful connections that inspire growth, creativity, and shared visions for the future.

Scorpio
16 January 2026

Scorpio, your inner world is illuminated today. The cosmos urges you to slow down and reconnect with your spiritual core. Secrets, dreams, or subtle insights may surface—pay attention. This is a good day for meditation, journaling, or simply resting in stillness. Don't push for productivity; restoration is the real work now. Release what no longer supports you, especially hidden fears or self-doubt. By clearing old energy, you prepare space for renewal. Trust the quiet, Scorpio—it holds the answers your busy mind has been seeking. Listen closely.

Affirmation & Gratitude

I honor rest and reflection, grateful for inner guidance that clears away fear and nurtures my spiritual renewal today.

Scorpio
17 January 2026

Scorpio, fresh energy surges as the Sun aligns with Pluto, your ruling planet. This day carries potent transformation energy. You may feel an intense urge to take control or reshape an area of your life. Channel this power constructively—avoid forcing outcomes. Instead, focus on intentional changes in career, habits, or relationships. Conversations today may reveal hidden truths, empowering you to act with clarity. This is a turning point, reminding you of your resilience and capacity for rebirth. Stand tall in your authenticity and watch doors begin to open.

Affirmation & Gratitude

I am grateful for transformation, embracing change with courage and trusting my power to reshape life with authenticity.

Scorpio
18 January 2026

Scorpio, today shines a spotlight on finances and resources. The cosmos encourages practicality—review budgets, investments, or spending habits. You may feel the temptation for indulgence, but long-term security matters more. A financial discussion or decision could surface, giving you a chance to assert your worth. Beyond money, this is also about valuing your time and energy. Don't undersell yourself. Recognize your skills as resources too. Small adjustments now will ripple into abundance later. Trust yourself to make grounded, empowered choices—your future self will thank you.

Affirmation & Gratitude

I give thanks for abundance in all forms, honoring my worth by making choices that build lasting stability and prosperity.

Scorpio
19 January 2026

Scorpio, communication is your superpower today. The stars encourage you to share your ideas, whether through writing, speaking, or teaching. You may also uncover important information that shifts your perspective. Be curious and open. This is an excellent day for networking, reaching out, or starting meaningful conversations. Your words carry influence, so use them wisely and compassionately. If conflict arises, your ability to see beneath the surface will help diffuse tension. Trust your instincts—what you say today could plant seeds that flourish long into the future.

Affirmation & Gratitude

I am grateful for my voice, sharing thoughts with clarity and compassion, planting seeds of connection and wisdom today.

Scorpio
20 January 2026

Scorpio, the Sun moves into Aquarius today, shifting your focus toward home and foundations. This is about redefining what stability means to you. You may feel the urge to rearrange your environment or strengthen family ties. Old memories may resurface, offering lessons for how you build security now. The energy supports grounding rituals—cleaning, decluttering, or even starting a fresh project at home. By creating a supportive base, you strengthen your capacity to pursue bigger goals. Trust that tending your roots nourishes your future growth.

Affirmation & Gratitude

I give thanks for my home and foundation, creating space that supports peace, strength, and growth in my journey.

Scorpio
21 January 2026

Scorpio, today the cosmos emphasizes creativity and joy. Venus enhances your charm, drawing attention in both love and social connections. Playful energy surrounds you—allow yourself to lean into fun without guilt. This is also a fertile day for creative projects, so channel passion into something expressive. Romance feels magnetic, yet meaningful—don't shy from showing affection. The lesson today is balance: seriousness isn't always required; joy is powerful too. By embracing play, you recharge your spirit and attract opportunities naturally.

Affirmation & Gratitude

I welcome joy with gratitude, expressing creativity and love freely, and allowing happiness to fuel my spirit and connections.

Scorpio
22 January 2026

Scorpio, the Moon highlights daily routines and health. Focus on balance—small, consistent habits now create major future results. Prioritize self-care, rest, and nourishing routines. At work, discipline brings rewards. Don't neglect emotional wellbeing—stress relief is essential. Real strength lies in aligning body, mind, and spirit.

Affirmation & Gratitude

I am grateful for my health, honoring my body and mind with nurturing habits that support strength, balance, and vitality daily.

Scorpio
23 January 2026

Scorpio, relationships demand attention today. Conversations may feel intense, but honesty strengthens bonds. Avoid control—listen with openness instead. Transformation happens when vulnerability meets patience. This day invites deepening love or resetting balance in partnerships. Focus on building respect, understanding, and trust.

Affirmation & Gratitude

I welcome gratitude in my relationships, embracing honesty, respect, and balance to create lasting and meaningful connections filled with love.

Scorpio
24 January 2026

Scorpio, career energy intensifies as opportunities for recognition arise. Step forward confidently; your efforts don't go unnoticed. Avoid impatience—slow, steady progress ensures lasting results. Authority figures may appreciate your persistence. Clarity about your purpose also surfaces today—trust your instincts and focus on long-term goals.

Affirmation & Gratitude

I give thanks for opportunities to grow in my career, embracing purpose, confidence, and persistence that lead to lasting success.

Scorpio
25 January 2026

Scorpio, the cosmos encourages rest and introspection today. Pay attention to dreams or subtle messages—they reveal hidden truths. Slow down, reflect, and replenish energy. This is a day for spiritual practices or journaling. Rest isn't retreat—it's preparation for transformation.

Affirmation & Gratitude

I honor gratitude for stillness and reflection, trusting my inner guidance to restore clarity, energy, and wisdom for the future.

Scorpio
26 January 2026

Scorpio, friendships and social connections come into focus. Group activities may inspire fresh ideas. Surround yourself with those who uplift and motivate. Collaboration creates opportunity. Discern who aligns with your values—boundaries protect your energy. Share your vision with confidence, and allies will support you.

Affirmation & Gratitude

I am grateful for inspiring friendships and supportive networks, welcoming collaboration and shared vision that expand growth and opportunity.

Scorpio
27 January 2026

Scorpio, today the Moon activates your inner world. Intuition is heightened—listen closely. Secrets, insights, or realizations emerge. Spend time in solitude for clarity. This isn't a day for rushing but for inner recalibration. Release outdated beliefs; they no longer serve your transformation.

Affirmation & Gratitude

I embrace gratitude for inner wisdom, trusting intuition to guide me toward clarity, release, and renewal on my transformative path.

Scorpio
28 January 2026

Scorpio, transformation energy peaks. Pluto empowers you to reshape areas of life where you've felt restricted. Focus on intentional change, not force. Take bold steps toward freedom—whether in habits, relationships, or career. Authenticity is your compass; follow it unapologetically. Renewal begins with your choice today.

Affirmation & Gratitude

I give thanks for transformation, embracing courage, authenticity, and renewal as I reshape my life with strength and clarity today.

Scorpio
29 January 2026

Scorpio, today shines a light on communication and connections. Mercury amplifies your voice—this is an excellent day to speak your truth. Don't hold back, but choose compassion in delivery. Important news, documents, or conversations may surface, shaping your plans ahead. Pay attention to details; clarity is key. A sibling, friend, or colleague could play a significant role today, reminding you that collaboration is as valuable as independence. Words carry power—use them to open doors, not close them.

Affirmation & Gratitude

I am grateful for my voice, choosing words of honesty and compassion that inspire trust, connection, and growth in others.

Scorpio
30 January 2026

Scorpio, home and family matters come into focus today. The Moon highlights your foundations, asking you to nurture what supports your stability. Domestic projects, conversations with loved ones, or even revisiting family memories may arise. Use this energy to strengthen bonds or bring peace to your personal sanctuary. Creating balance in your environment restores inner calm. Don't underestimate small acts of care—a tidy space or heartfelt talk brings harmony. Your inner security is the foundation for everything else.

Affirmation & Gratitude

I give thanks for my home and loved ones, creating balance, peace, and warmth that nourish my heart and spirit.

Scorpio
31 January 2026

Scorpio, creativity and joy flow today. Venus and Jupiter align to amplify your natural magnetism, attracting attention in romance, friendships, or creative projects. Passion runs high—channel it into something inspiring. Romance feels playful yet meaningful, while hobbies or personal expression fuel your spirit. Children or youthful influences may also inspire laughter and fun. Don't shy away from joy—it's just as transformative as intensity. Lightness renews your energy and attracts blessings. Today is about celebrating life and allowing your inner fire to shine brightly.

Affirmation & Gratitude

I embrace gratitude for joy, passion, and creativity, letting lighthearted energy restore balance and attract love and inspiration today.

February 2026

Scorpio
01 February 2026

Scorpio, focus shifts to routines, health, and responsibilities. The cosmos urges you to realign habits with your long-term goals. This isn't about dramatic overhauls but sustainable choices—hydration, rest, mindful movement, and organized planning. Work matters may demand focus, but avoid burnout by pacing yourself. Practical details matter now—attend to them carefully. By refining daily practices, you build a stronger foundation for bigger achievements. Small steps repeated consistently create lasting transformation. Remember, discipline is a form of self-love.

Affirmation & Gratitude

I am grateful for balance and discipline, choosing small, consistent habits that strengthen my health, energy, and daily flow.

Scorpio
02 February 2026

Scorpio, relationships are highlighted today. Conversations may reveal deeper truths, bringing clarity in love or partnerships. If tension arises, see it as a chance to reset balance. Vulnerability leads to healing. If single, attraction feels magnetic, yet meaningful—trust the pull, but proceed with patience. Saturn reminds you that meaningful connections grow slowly and with care. Partnerships today carry transformative potential, whether romantic, professional, or platonic. By being authentic and attentive, you strengthen bonds that matter most.

Affirmation & Gratitude

I honor gratitude for love and connection, embracing honesty, patience, and balance that create meaningful, lasting relationships.

Scorpio
03 February 2026

Scorpio, career opportunities call. The Sun illuminates your professional zone, encouraging you to step into visibility. Recognition could come from authority figures or peers—don't hide your talents. Present yourself with confidence and integrity. If doubts arise, remember: your depth and determination make you stand out. Consider long-term goals—are you aligned with your purpose? Today's steps, even small ones, shape your reputation. Push forward with courage, but stay grounded. Authenticity is your secret to lasting success.

Affirmation & Gratitude

I am grateful for opportunities to shine, confidently stepping into my purpose and embracing recognition with integrity and authenticity.

Scorpio
04 February 2026

Scorpio, today invites introspection. The Moon activates your spiritual zone, encouraging rest and reflection. You may feel drawn to solitude, dreams, or intuitive practices. Pay attention to inner nudges—guidance comes subtly now, through symbols, feelings, or synchronicities. Let go of mental clutter. Stillness reveals clarity. Don't view slowing down as weakness—it restores your strength for what's ahead. Transformation is born in silence as much as in action. Trust your inner compass—it knows the way forward.

Affirmation & Gratitude

I embrace gratitude for inner guidance, trusting rest and reflection to restore wisdom, energy, and clarity for the path ahead.

Scorpio
05 February 2026

Scorpio, social energy surrounds you today. Friends, groups, or communities may present opportunities that inspire growth. Collaboration is powerful now—share your vision with confidence. A conversation could spark a new idea or pathway. Still, use discernment: not every invitation aligns with your deeper purpose. Invest energy in circles that uplift and support you. By contributing authentically, you'll attract allies who help you manifest your goals. Today, connection is the bridge between dreams and action.

Affirmation & Gratitude

I am grateful for supportive connections, choosing to share my vision with allies who inspire growth, joy, and expansion.

Scorpio
06 February 2026

Scorpio, the Moon draws you inward, urging you to rest, reflect, and recharge. Intuition is heightened—pay attention to dreams, synchronicities, or inner whispers. Don't push yourself outwardly; this is a day for spiritual clarity. Release self-doubt or fears that have lingered. Rest restores balance, preparing you for bigger steps ahead. Time alone isn't isolation—it's sacred space for renewal. Trust the stillness, Scorpio; answers reveal themselves in silence.

Affirmation & Gratitude

I honor stillness with gratitude, trusting rest and inner wisdom to restore clarity, strength, and balance for my path ahead.

Scorpio
07 February 2026

Scorpio, transformation energy peaks as Pluto aligns with the Sun. You may feel powerful urges to reshape aspects of life—career, relationships, or self-belief. Channel intensity into constructive change, not control. Authenticity is your compass; follow it boldly. Hidden truths may surface, revealing what must be released. This is a rebirth moment—step into your power with conviction. By embracing change willingly, you open doors that once seemed locked.

Affirmation & Gratitude

I am grateful for transformation, courageously embracing change and trusting my authenticity to guide me toward freedom and renewal today.

Scorpio
08 February 2026

Scorpio, finances and resources take focus today. Review your budget, commitments, or long-term plans. Practical steps toward stability now pay off later. You may feel tempted by indulgence, but discipline strengthens your future security. Recognize your worth—don't settle for less. This is also about valuing your time and skills. By respecting your resources, you set the tone for abundance. Align choices with long-term goals, not fleeting desires.

Affirmation & Gratitude

I give thanks for abundance, honoring my worth and making empowered choices that create lasting stability and prosperity in my life.

Scorpio
09 February 2026

Scorpio, communication flows easily today. Expect lively exchanges, new ideas, or important news that clarifies your next steps. Your voice carries influence—use it to inspire or resolve. Writing, teaching, or speaking is favored. Stay curious; learning something new could unlock hidden potential. Siblings, neighbors, or colleagues may play a role in today's insights. Your words can build bridges, heal divides, and plant seeds for future opportunities. Speak with both passion and care.

Affirmation & Gratitude

I am grateful for my voice, using clarity and compassion in communication to inspire connection, understanding, and positive growth.

Scorpio
10 February 2026

Scorpio, home and family themes are highlighted. The cosmos asks you to nurture your foundations. Domestic responsibilities may require attention, or conversations with loved ones could bring healing. Consider ways to create harmony within your environment—decluttering, decorating, or simply spending quality time with family. Emotional security is essential to your strength; tending to it empowers every other area of life. Today is about grounding yourself in what feels safe, warm, and true.

Affirmation & Gratitude

I honor gratitude for home and family, creating peace, warmth, and balance in my environment to support inner stability.

Scorpio
11 February 2026

Scorpio, joy and creativity return today. The Moon amplifies playfulness, reminding you not to take everything so seriously. Passion flows strongly—romantic sparks, artistic expression, or laughter with friends uplift your spirit. Allow yourself to lean into activities that excite you. Fun is a healer, Scorpio, and lighthearted energy replenishes your strength for the deeper work ahead. Embrace spontaneity—you'll discover inspiration hiding in joy. Celebrate life today with open arms.

Affirmation & Gratitude

I embrace gratitude for joy, allowing creativity, love, and playfulness to brighten my spirit and attract inspiration today.

Scorpio
12 February 2026

Scorpio, the cosmos highlights routines, wellness, and responsibilities. Focus on how your daily actions align with long-term goals. Small adjustments create big change. Health matters need attention—choose habits that fuel energy instead of depleting it. Work tasks may feel demanding, but discipline will see you through. Balance duty with rest to avoid burnout. Today reminds you: transformation comes not from drastic leaps, but from consistent, intentional steps that support your wellbeing and purpose.

Affirmation & Gratitude

I am grateful for the strength to create balance, making choices that nurture health, discipline, and long-term success daily.

Scorpio
13 February 2026

Scorpio, relationships move into focus. Venus stirs both passion and honesty—be willing to express your true feelings. Tension may arise, but it's an opportunity to clarify boundaries or deepen trust. Single Scorpios may feel drawn toward magnetic connections, though Saturn insists on patience and maturity. Authenticity is key. Love strengthens when it's rooted in respect and openness. Today asks you to show up fully, whether in romance, friendship, or professional partnerships. Connection thrives on courage.

Affirmation & Gratitude

I welcome gratitude for meaningful relationships, embracing honesty, patience, and balance that strengthen trust, love, and mutual respect.

Scorpio
14 February 2026

Scorpio, on this Valentine's Day, cosmic energy heightens your romantic and creative spark. Whether partnered or single, the stars urge you to celebrate love in all forms—self-love, friendship, or passion. Your magnetism is undeniable, drawing others toward your depth. Creative expression also flourishes, so indulge in activities that ignite joy. Avoid overcomplicating feelings—sometimes love is simply about presence, laughter, and shared moments. Today is about choosing joy, connection, and gratitude for love in its many forms.

Affirmation & Gratitude

I am grateful for love in all its expressions, celebrating joy, connection, and creativity that nourish my heart and spirit.

Scorpio
15 February 2026

Scorpio, career and public image are emphasized today. Recognition is possible if you've been consistent with your efforts. Step into the spotlight with confidence—your integrity and depth will shine. Conversations with leaders or mentors may open doors, so present yourself clearly. Don't shrink from responsibility; you're more than capable. Ask yourself if your current path truly aligns with your purpose. This is your chance to realign ambitions with authenticity. Bold steps bring long-lasting rewards.

Affirmation & Gratitude

I give thanks for opportunities to grow in my career, stepping forward with courage, integrity, and alignment to my true purpose.

Scorpio
16 February 2026

Scorpio, the cosmos draws you inward for reflection. The Moon emphasizes intuition and dreams—messages from your subconscious may be strong now. Don't ignore them. This is a day to step back, rest, and process emotions quietly. Avoid forcing progress; wisdom arises in stillness. Release what you've been clinging to—whether fear, doubt, or old stories. Transformation requires space, and today offers exactly that. By embracing quiet moments, you restore clarity and prepare for the next breakthrough.

Affirmation & Gratitude

I honor gratitude for inner wisdom, trusting rest, stillness, and reflection to guide me toward clarity and renewal today.

Scorpio
17 February 2026

Scorpio, friendships and social circles take priority. Group efforts or connections could inspire exciting opportunities. Share your ideas—collaboration multiplies your impact. Still, be mindful of where you invest energy. Choose relationships that uplift and empower you, not ones that drain. A friend's perspective may spark a new way of seeing your situation. Networking today plants seeds for future projects. The stars remind you: community is a catalyst, but discernment protects your energy.

Affirmation & Gratitude

I am grateful for uplifting connections, embracing collaboration and community while choosing relationships that align with my values and growth.

Scorpio
18 February 2026

Scorpio, the Sun shifts into Pisces, energizing your creative and romantic sector. This is a fertile time for inspiration, joy, and love. Artistic pursuits flow easily, and your intuition shines through creative outlets. In relationships, passion deepens, but so does your need for emotional honesty. Celebrate what makes you feel alive—fun, beauty, love, and playful exploration. By embracing creativity, you not only recharge your spirit but also attract opportunities that feel aligned with your soul.

Affirmation & Gratitude

I give thanks for joy, creativity, and passion, embracing love and inspiration that brighten my heart and guide my path.

Scorpio
19 February 2026

Scorpio, today highlights your daily routines and health. The stars ask you to refine habits—small adjustments now build lasting transformation. Pay attention to body signals; rest if needed, nourish wisely, and move with intention. Work demands may feel heavy, but clarity comes when you prioritize what matters. Don't overextend—balance responsibility with self-care. Today's energy teaches that true strength comes from sustainable rhythm, not burnout. Commit to habits that honor your wellbeing and long-term growth.

Affirmation & Gratitude

I am grateful for my health and routines, making choices today that nurture energy, focus, balance, and long-term vitality.

Scorpio
20 February 2026

Scorpio, partnership energy intensifies. Conversations may test boundaries, but they offer opportunities for honesty and growth. Whether in love or professional settings, today calls for patience and mutual respect. Mars fuels passion, while Saturn demands responsibility—blend both for balance. If single, attraction may feel magnetic, but clarity matters more than chemistry. Real connection requires authenticity, and you're ready to show up fully. Relationships transform when you lead with openness, not control.

Affirmation & Gratitude

I am grateful for meaningful relationships, choosing honesty, patience, and respect that deepen love, trust, and connection today.

Scorpio
21 February 2026

Scorpio, career matters gain momentum. Recognition may arrive, or new responsibilities could highlight your leadership skills. Authority figures take notice—be prepared to step forward confidently. This is a day to align ambition with integrity. Avoid shortcuts—lasting success comes from authenticity and persistence. If doubts arise, remind yourself you're capable and resilient. Career shifts or opportunities today may set the tone for months ahead. The cosmos asks you to own your power gracefully.

Affirmation & Gratitude

I give thanks for career opportunities, stepping into visibility with courage, authenticity, and confidence to build lasting success.

Scorpio
22 February 2026

Scorpio, today brings spiritual renewal. The Moon highlights intuition, encouraging rest, reflection, and listening within. Dreams or synchronicities may reveal answers. Avoid rushing decisions—clarity comes from stillness. Emotions may feel heightened; give yourself grace to process them. Spiritual practices, journaling, or simply sitting in silence will refresh your energy. This is not a day for outward pushing but for recalibration. Trust that the quiet work today builds strength for tomorrow's transformation.

Affirmation & Gratitude

I honor rest and gratitude for inner guidance, trusting silence and reflection to reveal clarity, healing, and renewal today.

Scorpio
23 February 2026

Scorpio, friendships and community connections are highlighted. You may feel drawn toward social gatherings or collaborative projects. Inspiration arises through group discussions or shared vision. Still, choose your circles wisely—invest energy in people who align with your values. A friend may bring unexpected support or insight. Networking today plants seeds for future opportunity. Your path expands when you allow others to walk alongside you.

Affirmation & Gratitude

I am grateful for supportive friendships, embracing collaboration and community that inspire creativity, growth, and meaningful shared opportunities.

Scorpio
24 February 2026

Scorpio, creative energy flows strongly. The Sun in Pisces amplifies your artistic, playful, and romantic spirit. Express yourself freely—whether through art, writing, or deep conversations. Relationships thrive when you share joy without fear. Children or lighthearted influences may remind you to reconnect with fun. Don't dismiss playfulness; it restores balance and renews inspiration. Today is about letting your heart guide your choices. Trust joy as much as intensity—it has transformative power too.

Affirmation & Gratitude

I embrace gratitude for joy and creativity, allowing play, love, and inspiration to guide my spirit and renew energy.

Scorpio
25 February 2026

Scorpio, focus shifts to practical matters—health, work, and organization. The Moon highlights areas that need structure. Tidy your environment, review your schedule, or streamline routines. Even small improvements boost productivity and wellbeing. At work, your attention to detail shines; others notice your dedication. Don't neglect rest, though—burnout dims your brilliance. By creating order in the small things, you free energy for bigger goals. Balance responsibility with self-care.

Affirmation & Gratitude

I give thanks for order and balance, creating healthy routines that support clarity, productivity, and sustained energy today.

Scorpio
26 February 2026

Scorpio, partnerships are emphasized today. The stars highlight balance in love, business, or close friendships. Conversations may uncover truths you've avoided—see them as opportunities to grow, not conflicts. If single, attraction feels magnetic, but discern whether it aligns with your deeper needs. Today teaches that real intimacy thrives on honesty and patience, not control. By allowing others to meet you halfway, you strengthen trust and respect in all your bonds.

Affirmation & Gratitude

I am grateful for the gift of connection, choosing honesty and patience to build stronger, more balanced relationships today.

Scorpio
27 February 2026

Scorpio, career and reputation gain focus today. You may feel pressure to prove yourself, but the cosmos urges steady confidence, not overexertion. Recognition is possible if you've been consistent, while new opportunities may surface through authority figures or mentors. Step into visibility with authenticity—your depth and determination speak louder than any performance. Ask yourself: does your current direction truly reflect your purpose? Real success is rooted in alignment, not just achievement.

Affirmation & Gratitude

I give thanks for opportunities to grow in my career, stepping forward with courage, integrity, and alignment to purpose.

Scorpio
28 February 2026

Scorpio, the Moon draws you inward for reflection. This is a day to restore energy, connect with your intuition, and let go of lingering doubts. Don't push yourself outwardly—listen instead to what your spirit needs most. Dreams or signs may deliver insight, so keep a journal close. Rest, meditation, or simply enjoying silence refreshes your resilience. Release what's outdated; clarity emerges when you create space for it. Transformation often begins quietly, beneath the surface.

Affirmation & Gratitude

I honor gratitude for rest and renewal, trusting stillness and intuition to guide me toward clarity and strength today.

March
2026

Scorpio
01 March 2026

Scorpio, friendships and community bring inspiration. The cosmos reminds you that collaboration opens doors. Group activities or conversations may spark ideas for the future. Surround yourself with uplifting influences; avoid those who drain energy. Today's connections may lead to opportunities in months ahead. By sharing your vision with others, you attract allies who align with your goals. Trust that your network is part of your growth path.

Affirmation & Gratitude

I am grateful for inspiring friendships and supportive connections, embracing collaboration that expands opportunity, creativity, and growth.

Scorpio
02 March 2026

Scorpio, creativity and romance surge as the Sun amplifies your playful, passionate side. Express yourself freely—through art, writing, or love. Romantic energy feels magnetic, though honesty and presence matter more than intensity. Joy is transformative; don't underestimate the healing power of laughter and lightheartedness. Children or creative projects may also inspire you. Allow yourself to enjoy beauty without guilt. Today is about celebrating what makes your spirit feel alive.

Affirmation & Gratitude

I embrace gratitude for joy, creativity, and passion, allowing playful energy to renew my heart and spirit today.

Scorpio
03 March 2026

Scorpio, focus shifts to routines, health, and productivity. The Moon urges structure and discipline—review your schedule and refine your habits. Even small adjustments bring big results. At work, your sharp focus is noticed, though remember balance: self-care is as important as deadlines. Sustainable progress comes from aligning responsibility with rest. Today is about building stability in the small details that shape your bigger goals. Order brings strength and clarity.

Affirmation & Gratitude

I give thanks for balance and structure, creating habits that nurture health, clarity, and productivity in my daily life.

Scorpio
04 March 2026

Scorpio, relationships take center stage again. Venus emphasizes both passion and harmony, urging you to lean into authentic connection. Tension may highlight areas where compromise is needed—don't resist it. Transformation occurs when vulnerability meets respect. Single Scorpios may attract someone deeply aligned with their spirit. In partnerships, today's honesty can strengthen bonds. Remember, true intimacy grows when both hearts are open. Lead with presence, and love will naturally deepen.

Affirmation & Gratitude

I am grateful for love and connection, choosing honesty, presence, and respect to build deeper and more authentic relationships.

Scorpio
05 March 2026

Scorpio, today highlights your career and public image. Recognition is possible, but only if you've been consistent in your efforts. A mentor or authority figure could offer advice or opportunity. Don't shrink from responsibility—you're more than capable. Step into visibility with authenticity, not ego. This is a day for aligning ambition with integrity, ensuring your goals reflect your true purpose. Your professional path strengthens when you lead with depth and conviction.

Affirmation & Gratitude

I am grateful for career opportunities, stepping into visibility with authenticity, courage, and purpose to achieve lasting success today.

Scorpio
06 March 2026

Scorpio, the Moon draws you inward. Intuition is strong today, guiding you through dreams, synchronicities, or subtle nudges. Pay attention. Rest and reflection are more productive than pushing forward. Release outdated habits or fears that keep you from progress. Time in solitude helps you recalibrate and find clarity. Today, transformation begins within—trust the whispers of your soul. By slowing down, you prepare yourself for greater breakthroughs on the horizon.

Affirmation & Gratitude

I honor gratitude for stillness and inner wisdom, trusting my intuition to guide me toward clarity, renewal, and strength.

Scorpio
07 March 2026

Scorpio, friendships and community ties are emphasized. A group conversation or shared activity may spark inspiration for future goals. Collaboration carries potential—don't underestimate the power of connection. Still, discern where your energy flows; invest in uplifting circles that align with your values. A friend's perspective could shift how you see a current situation. By engaging with community, you not only expand your network but also reaffirm your role as a source of wisdom.

Affirmation & Gratitude

I am grateful for supportive friendships and communities, choosing collaboration and shared vision that inspire growth and opportunity.

Scorpio
08 March 2026

Scorpio, creativity and romance flourish today. Venus amplifies your charm, making you magnetic in love and inspiring in creative pursuits. Passion runs high—lean into it with honesty. Joy and playfulness restore balance and remind you that life is not all intensity. If partnered, deepen bonds with shared fun. If single, your magnetism attracts admirers. Creative projects also flow easily. Today is about celebrating what makes you feel alive—love, art, and laughter.

Affirmation & Gratitude

I embrace gratitude for joy, creativity, and passion, allowing playful energy to renew my heart and inspire my spirit.

Scorpio
09 March 2026

Scorpio, routines and wellness come into focus. The cosmos asks you to assess your daily habits—are they fueling your energy or draining it? Small shifts now create lasting results. Prioritize hydration, movement, and organization. Work tasks may feel pressing, but efficiency improves when you balance responsibility with self-care. Sustainable progress grows from structure, not overexertion. Commit to routines that align with your wellbeing and future goals. Today, discipline is your ally.

Affirmation & Gratitude

I am grateful for balance in routines, creating healthy habits that support my energy, clarity, and long-term success.

Scorpio
10 March 2026

Scorpio, partnerships are highlighted again. Conversations may reveal truths, testing your honesty and patience. Lean into openness—vulnerability leads to stronger connections. Passion is present, but Saturn reminds you that responsibility matters as much as desire. Single Scorpios may feel drawn toward magnetic attraction, but time will reveal true alignment. Today's energy teaches that authentic bonds grow through respect and balanced effort. Lead with empathy; relationships will deepen naturally.

Affirmation & Gratitude

I am grateful for meaningful relationships, choosing honesty, respect, and patience to nurture love and trust in all connections.

Scorpio
11 March 2026

Scorpio, career momentum builds today. Authority figures may recognize your effort, or opportunities may appear unexpectedly. The stars ask you to align ambition with authenticity. Be bold, but not reckless—success rooted in integrity lasts. If doubts creep in, trust your resilience. This is a day to claim your power, remembering that your purpose isn't just achievement but influence that uplifts others. Step forward with confidence; you're ready for more.

Affirmation & Gratitude

I give thanks for recognition and purpose, stepping forward with confidence and authenticity to create meaningful success in my career.

Scorpio
12 March 2026

Scorpio, today's energy emphasizes introspection. The Moon activates your spiritual sector, making intuition sharper than usual. Pay attention to subtle signs—dreams, numbers, or symbols. You may crave solitude, and that's exactly what you need to restore balance. This is not a day for outward pressure but for spiritual clarity. Meditation, journaling, or simply silence will reveal truths you've overlooked. Transformation begins in stillness, and today offers space to shed unnecessary weight.

Affirmation & Gratitude

I am grateful for inner wisdom and clarity, allowing stillness and intuition to guide me toward renewal and strength today.

Scorpio
13 March 2026

Scorpio, friendships and community highlight your day. Group connections may inspire fresh ideas or opportunities. Collaboration expands your vision—don't underestimate the power of shared goals. Still, discern carefully where to invest energy. Surround yourself with uplifting influences that align with your values. Someone in your circle could bring valuable advice or unexpected support. Remember, the right community isn't just company—it's a catalyst for your personal and professional growth.

Affirmation & Gratitude

I am grateful for inspiring friendships and supportive communities, choosing collaboration that uplifts and expands opportunities for growth and creativity.

Scorpio
14 March 2026

Scorpio, today creativity and joy flow freely. Venus and the Sun amplify your magnetism, drawing opportunities for romance, fun, and self-expression. Lean into hobbies, passions, or playful activities that make you feel alive. Romance deepens when you lead with authenticity and joy, not intensity. Creative projects may also bring breakthroughs. The cosmos reminds you that joy is not frivolous—it is fuel for transformation. Allow yourself space to celebrate life unapologetically.

Affirmation & Gratitude

I embrace gratitude for creativity and joy, allowing love, playfulness, and passion to uplift my heart and spirit today.

Scorpio
15 March 2026

Scorpio, focus shifts to work, wellness, and order. Responsibilities may feel heavy, but discipline helps you handle them with efficiency. This is a great day to organize, plan, or refine your routines. Health and productivity thrive when you align action with balance. Don't overextend—self-care ensures long-term success. The cosmos reminds you: transformation doesn't always come through intensity, but through consistent, mindful steps. Progress today strengthens your resilience for what's ahead.

Affirmation & Gratitude

I give thanks for balance in my daily life, choosing discipline and self-care to build strength, clarity, and stability.

Scorpio
16 March 2026

Scorpio, partnerships are highlighted. Conversations may test patience, but they bring opportunities for growth. Be open to hearing another's truth without defense. Whether in romance, friendships, or work, today teaches that vulnerability is strength. Passion is present, but long-term stability requires honesty and respect. For singles, attraction feels magnetic, yet time will reveal what's real. By leaning into openness, you strengthen the foundations of all your important connections.

Affirmation & Gratitude

I am grateful for love and connection, embracing honesty, openness, and patience to nurture deeper and more meaningful relationships.

Scorpio
17 March 2026

Scorpio, career energy is strong today. Recognition or opportunity may arrive, spotlighting your resilience and capability. Don't hold back from showcasing your strengths, but let humility guide you. Authenticity is what sets you apart. Mentors or authority figures may notice your dedication, opening doors for the future. This is a powerful day to align career goals with purpose. Your influence grows when you lead with wisdom and integrity.

Affirmation & Gratitude

I give thanks for opportunities in my career, stepping into visibility with courage, authenticity, and a clear sense of purpose.

Scorpio
18 March 2026

Scorpio, the cosmos asks you to rest and reflect. Emotional sensitivity is heightened, making this an ideal day for quiet renewal. Dreams or intuitive nudges may reveal truths you've overlooked. Release mental clutter and allow stillness to restore your clarity. Today's lesson is that growth doesn't always require constant movement—sometimes it's found in surrender. By honoring your inner world, you recharge and align with greater transformation ahead.

Affirmation & Gratitude

I honor gratitude for rest and reflection, trusting stillness and intuition to guide me toward clarity, peace, and renewal.

Scorpio
19 March 2026

Scorpio, friendships and community ties hold importance today. Group discussions may spark innovative ideas, while collaboration brings opportunities. The stars remind you that teamwork strengthens your vision. Still, remain discerning—don't give energy to circles that drain you. A friend may offer support or insight that helps you see a situation differently. Your role within your community may feel clearer now, reaffirming that your growth is not just individual but collective.

Affirmation & Gratitude

I am grateful for supportive friendships, embracing collaboration and community that inspire creativity, growth, and new shared opportunities.

Scorpio
20 March 2026

Scorpio, the Equinox shifts the Sun into Aries, energizing your daily routines and wellbeing. This cosmic shift asks you to review habits and realign health priorities. Fresh energy supports beginning new routines, whether fitness, organization, or mindful practices. Work matters gain momentum too, making this a great day to tackle lingering tasks. By refining your daily structure, you create balance and clarity for larger ambitions. Transformation begins in the details of everyday life.

Affirmation & Gratitude

I give thanks for renewed energy, creating daily routines that align with my health, productivity, and long-term growth.

Scorpio
21 March 2026

Scorpio, relationships intensify under today's cosmic alignment. Conversations may bring clarity, though emotions could run deep. Allow vulnerability—it builds trust. Whether romantic, platonic, or professional, honesty strengthens bonds. If single, attraction feels magnetic, but Saturn reminds you patience is necessary for lasting love. Lean into openness rather than control. Today's lessons teach that true partnership thrives when balance, respect, and empathy lead. This is a chance to reset or deepen important connections.

Affirmation & Gratitude

I honor gratitude for connection, embracing patience, honesty, and empathy that strengthen relationships and create authentic, lasting bonds.

Scorpio
22 March 2026

Scorpio, career matters come into focus. Recognition may arrive unexpectedly, or responsibility could increase. The stars encourage you to step forward with confidence. Align ambition with authenticity—success is strongest when it reflects your true calling. Authority figures may acknowledge your effort. If you've been questioning your path, today brings clarity. The cosmos asks you to own your influence without arrogance. By embodying integrity, you strengthen your reputation and open doors to future opportunity.

Affirmation & Gratitude

I am grateful for career opportunities, stepping into visibility with courage, purpose, and authenticity that build lasting success.

Scorpio
23 March 2026

Scorpio, introspection is emphasized. The Moon highlights your inner world, asking you to pause, reflect, and release. Pay attention to dreams or symbols—they hold guidance. Solitude brings clarity, so create space for rest and renewal. Avoid forcing progress; today is about clearing emotional clutter. By honoring stillness, you prepare for transformation ahead. Growth doesn't always happen loudly—it often begins in silence. The answers you seek are already within; listen carefully today.

Affirmation & Gratitude

I give thanks for stillness and intuition, trusting quiet reflection to guide me toward clarity, renewal, and inner strength.

Scorpio
24 March 2026

Scorpio, social connections and friendships bring energy today. Networking, group projects, or casual conversations may spark inspiration for your future goals. Surround yourself with uplifting company—your energy is too precious to waste on negativity. A friend's advice or encouragement could give you fresh perspective. Collaboration fuels growth, and today shows that shared vision amplifies opportunity. By aligning with community, you expand your influence and gain momentum for your personal path.

Affirmation & Gratitude

I am grateful for inspiring friendships, embracing collaboration and supportive networks that encourage creativity, growth, and opportunity.

Scorpio
25 March 2026

Scorpio, joy and creativity flow naturally today. The stars encourage you to explore hobbies, passions, or playful romance. Venus highlights your charm, making you magnetic in relationships and inspiring in self-expression. Don't underestimate the healing power of fun—it recharges your spirit. Allow yourself to celebrate beauty and laughter without guilt. Creative breakthroughs are possible now, offering fresh inspiration. Today is about reconnecting with what makes you feel alive and vibrant.

Affirmation & Gratitude

I embrace gratitude for joy, love, and creativity, allowing passion and playfulness to uplift my spirit and renew my energy.

Scorpio
26 March 2026

Scorpio, work and wellness themes take priority today. The cosmos urges you to refine routines and manage responsibilities with balance. Pay attention to your body—nourish, hydrate, and rest where needed. At work, efficiency and focus bring progress. Avoid perfectionism; consistency is more valuable than control. This is a day for grounding, organizing, and clearing space for productivity. By honoring your wellbeing alongside duty, you create sustainable energy for future achievements.

Affirmation & Gratitude

I am grateful for balance in my routines, choosing discipline and self-care that strengthen clarity, health, and long-term progress.

Scorpio
27 March 2026

Scorpio, relationships take the spotlight. Conversations may bring hidden truths to the surface, requiring patience and honesty. Lean into vulnerability—it strengthens bonds. Passion is present, yet Saturn reminds you that responsibility and respect are the foundations of lasting love. If single, attraction may feel magnetic, but time reveals alignment. Today's energy asks you to prioritize authenticity over control, creating partnerships built on mutual trust. Real intimacy grows when both hearts remain open.

Affirmation & Gratitude

I give thanks for meaningful relationships, embracing honesty, respect, and openness to deepen love, trust, and connection today.

Scorpio
28 March 2026

Scorpio, career momentum builds strongly. Recognition may come from your dedication, or opportunities for advancement could present themselves. Authority figures notice your persistence, and your influence grows when you lead authentically. Align ambition with purpose—this ensures success that lasts. Doubt may whisper, but your resilience outweighs it. Be bold but humble. Today is about owning your capability and stepping into visibility. The stars remind you: your work is not just action, it's legacy.

Affirmation & Gratitude

I am grateful for opportunities to grow in my career, stepping forward with courage, authenticity, and purpose for lasting success.

Scorpio
29 March 2026

Scorpio, the Moon highlights your inner world. Emotions may feel tender, urging you to pause and reflect. Solitude provides clarity—listen to your intuition and let go of what weighs you down. This is not a day for pushing outward, but for rebalancing inward. Pay attention to dreams, synchronicities, or subtle feelings—they hold answers. Growth often begins in stillness. By restoring your inner world, you prepare for the next cycle of transformation.

Affirmation & Gratitude

I honor gratitude for rest and reflection, trusting inner guidance to reveal clarity, strength, and renewal today.

Scorpio
30 March 2026

Scorpio, friendships and group connections bring opportunities. Networking, social circles, or shared projects could inspire new paths forward. Collaboration is powerful—allow others to add perspective. Still, choose carefully where you invest energy; your time is precious. A friend's encouragement may shift how you view a challenge. Today's lesson is that you don't need to walk your path alone—community adds strength. Trust in supportive alliances that align with your spirit.

Affirmation & Gratitude

I am grateful for inspiring friendships, embracing collaboration and shared vision that expand growth, creativity, and opportunity.

Scorpio
31 March 2026

Scorpio, creative and romantic energy flows freely. Venus enhances your charm, making you magnetic in love and expressive in artistic pursuits. Passion runs high—use it to deepen relationships or fuel creative breakthroughs. Don't underestimate the healing power of joy; fun restores balance. Explore what makes your spirit feel alive—whether through hobbies, laughter, or love. Today is about celebrating beauty and connection without guilt. By honoring joy, you attract more blessings.

Affirmation & Gratitude

I embrace gratitude for love, creativity, and joy, allowing passion and play to uplift and inspire my spirit.

April
2026

Scorpio
01 April 2026

Scorpio, the Sun and Moon emphasize routines and health. This is a day to refine structure, balance responsibilities, and care for your body. Small, consistent actions—like hydration, rest, or organization—yield powerful long-term results. Work requires discipline, but avoid burnout by pacing yourself. Transformation comes not from drastic leaps, but from sustainable habits. Today's energy helps you reset routines and create balance. By honoring your wellbeing, you set the stage for success ahead.

Affirmation & Gratitude

I am grateful for balance and discipline, creating healthy habits that support energy, clarity, and stability in my daily life.

Scorpio
02 April 2026

Scorpio, relationships are emphasized today. The stars bring conversations that could clarify boundaries or deepen intimacy. Passion is present, yet lasting connections require patience and honesty. If tension arises, see it as a chance for renewal, not conflict. For singles, magnetic attraction may appear—trust your instincts. Partnerships thrive when you lead with empathy rather than control. The cosmos reminds you that true intimacy is built on respect, vulnerability, and balance.

Affirmation & Gratitude

I give thanks for meaningful connections, embracing patience, honesty, and empathy to create stronger, more authentic relationships today.

Scorpio
03 April 2026

Scorpio, career energy intensifies. Recognition or new opportunities may emerge, spotlighting your dedication. Step confidently into visibility; your efforts are noticed. The key is authenticity—success aligned with your purpose has lasting value. Avoid rushing or chasing validation; your depth already sets you apart. Authority figures may offer support, or a mentor could guide you. Today is about aligning ambition with legacy. Own your capability without arrogance.

Affirmation & Gratitude

I am grateful for opportunities to shine, stepping into visibility with courage, authenticity, and integrity that build lasting success.

Scorpio
04 April 2026

Scorpio, the Moon draws you inward. Emotions may feel heightened, urging reflection and rest. Pay attention to dreams or subtle intuitive nudges—they hold guidance. This is a day to let go of what no longer serves you, whether fears or outdated habits. Quiet practices like journaling, meditation, or time in nature will refresh your clarity. Transformation often begins in silence, and today offers space for deep inner release and renewal.

Affirmation & Gratitude

I honor gratitude for rest and reflection, trusting stillness and intuition to restore clarity, healing, and strength within me.

Scorpio
05 April 2026

Scorpio, friendships and community connections are highlighted. Shared activities, networking, or conversations may spark new ideas. Surround yourself with people who support and uplift you. Collaboration today carries potential for future projects or opportunities. A friend may offer advice or encouragement that shifts your outlook. The stars remind you that community helps expand your vision. Discern where your energy flows —invest it only where there is mutual respect and alignment.

Affirmation & Gratitude

I am grateful for inspiring friendships, embracing collaboration and community that expand creativity, growth, and opportunity.

Scorpio
06 April 2026

Scorpio, creativity and joy flow strongly today. Venus highlights your playful side, making this an excellent day for romance, self-expression, and artistic pursuits. Love feels magnetic, but authenticity matters more than intensity. Engage in hobbies or passions that make your spirit feel alive. Children or youthful energy may also bring inspiration. Joy is not frivolous—it is transformative. Today, celebrate beauty, laughter, and love without guilt.

Affirmation & Gratitude

I embrace gratitude for creativity, joy, and love, allowing playful energy to uplift and inspire my spirit today.

Scorpio
07 April 2026

Scorpio, health and routines come into focus. The cosmos urges you to refine daily habits for balance and stability. Small changes, such as organization, better nutrition, or mindful rest, create long-lasting transformation. At work, your efficiency is noticed, though avoid burnout by pacing yourself. This is a day to ground yourself in sustainable practices. Remember, discipline is a form of self-love.

Affirmation & Gratitude

I give thanks for healthy routines and balance, creating daily habits that support energy, clarity, and long-term wellbeing.

Scorpio
08 April 2026

Scorpio, relationships take center stage again. The stars amplify your ability to build intimacy, but only if you embrace openness. Conversations may feel intense, yet they offer breakthroughs. Be honest about what you need, and listen just as deeply. Love deepens through patience and respect. For singles, attraction is likely, though alignment matters more than desire. The cosmos reminds you: real connection flourishes when authenticity leads.

Affirmation & Gratitude

I am grateful for love and connection, choosing honesty, respect, and patience to nurture deeper bonds today.

Scorpio
09 April 2026

Scorpio, career momentum grows. Authority figures may recognize your persistence, or new responsibilities could open fresh paths. The stars encourage you to align ambition with authenticity. Avoid chasing recognition alone—lasting success comes when it reflects your soul's truth. Opportunities may surface unexpectedly; be ready to step forward. Present yourself confidently, but remain humble. Today is about planting seeds that shape your professional future. Your influence strengthens when you lead with integrity and depth.

Affirmation & Gratitude

I am grateful for career recognition, embracing authenticity and courage while stepping into opportunities that align with my true purpose.

Scorpio
10 April 2026

Scorpio, introspection takes the spotlight. The Moon pulls you inward, urging you to rest, release, and reconnect with your intuition. Emotional sensitivity may heighten, but this isn't weakness—it's clarity. Trust dreams, symbols, and inner whispers; they hold guidance for your next step. Avoid overextending outwardly; this is a day for healing and spiritual renewal. By letting go of emotional clutter, you prepare space for transformation. Stillness reveals answers waiting to be heard.

Affirmation & Gratitude

I honor gratitude for stillness and reflection, trusting inner wisdom to bring clarity, healing, and renewal today.

Scorpio
11 April 2026

Scorpio, friendships and social connections energize you today. Networking, group projects, or even casual conversations may spark inspiring ideas. Collaboration is a theme —teamwork multiplies your vision. Still, protect your boundaries; not everyone deserves your time. A friend's encouragement or advice may give you new perspective. Today reminds you that you don't have to walk alone —community adds strength to your journey. Choose uplifting company, and watch new opportunities grow.

Affirmation & Gratitude

I am grateful for supportive friendships and shared visions, embracing collaboration that inspires creativity, growth, and future opportunity.

Scorpio
12 April 2026

Scorpio, the cosmos amplifies creativity and joy. Venus enhances your charm, drawing attention in romance or artistic pursuits. Passion runs high, but presence matters more than intensity. This is a day to explore hobbies, art, music, or laughter. Fun restores balance and attracts new inspiration. Love feels magnetic, but authenticity keeps it meaningful. Celebrate what makes your heart feel alive. Joy isn't an indulgence—it's a vital source of transformation. Lean into it unapologetically.

Affirmation & Gratitude

I embrace gratitude for joy, love, and creativity, allowing passion and playfulness to uplift and inspire my spirit.

Scorpio
13 April 2026

Scorpio, today emphasizes structure, work, and wellness. Review your routines—are they supporting or draining you? Small adjustments now create long-lasting improvement. Prioritize health and productivity by finding balance between effort and rest. Discipline is your ally, but don't neglect self-care. At work, efficiency and focus help you handle tasks with clarity. Today is about grounding yourself in practical habits that serve your bigger goals. Transformation grows through consistent, intentional steps forward.

Affirmation & Gratitude

I give thanks for balance in my daily routines, creating habits that nurture clarity, health, and sustainable progress.

Scorpio
14 April 2026

Scorpio, relationships move into focus. Conversations may reveal truths that shift dynamics. Tension can lead to breakthroughs if handled with honesty and patience. Whether in romance, friendship, or professional partnerships, today asks you to listen deeply and speak authentically. Vulnerability strengthens bonds. If single, attraction may feel powerful, but long-term alignment matters most. The stars remind you that true connection thrives on mutual respect, openness, and emotional balance.

Affirmation & Gratitude

I am grateful for love and connection, choosing honesty, patience, and empathy to nurture deeper and more authentic relationships.

Scorpio
15 April 2026

Scorpio, career and public image gain emphasis. Opportunities for recognition or advancement may surface, though patience is required for results to unfold. Align your ambition with your greater purpose—success rooted in authenticity lasts longer. Authority figures may take notice, so stay prepared. Doubts may arise, but trust your resilience and vision. Today is about stepping confidently into your path, remembering that influence is most powerful when guided by integrity and wisdom.

Affirmation & Gratitude

I give thanks for opportunities in my career, stepping into visibility with authenticity, confidence, and purpose today.

Scorpio
16 April 2026

Scorpio, today favors introspection. The Moon encourages quiet reflection, helping you release outdated beliefs or fears. Pay attention to dreams or symbols—they reveal truths waiting to surface. You may feel emotional sensitivity, but this is guidance, not weakness. Step back from busyness, focus on what restores balance. Spiritual practices or journaling offer clarity. Transformation starts within, and today offers space for that inner renewal. Trust your intuition—it leads the way.

Affirmation & Gratitude

I honor gratitude for stillness and reflection, trusting inner wisdom to clear away fear and guide renewal today.

Scorpio
17 April 2026

Scorpio, friendships and social networks hold importance today. A group activity, casual conversation, or connection could spark unexpected inspiration. Collaboration expands opportunity, but discern where you invest your energy—choose uplifting company. A friend's advice or encouragement may shift your perspective, reminding you of the power of community. Your role within your circle may feel clearer now, showing how your presence supports collective growth.

Affirmation & Gratitude

I am grateful for inspiring friendships and community, embracing collaboration that encourages growth, creativity, and shared vision today.

Scorpio
18 April 2026

Scorpio, creativity and romance surge under today's cosmic influence. Venus amplifies your charm, making you magnetic in love and expressive in art. Lean into hobbies, passions, or lighthearted joy. Relationships deepen when shared with playfulness, not just intensity. Children or youthful influences may inspire laughter. Remember, joy is transformative—it restores your spirit and opens doors. Today is about celebrating beauty, love, and fun without guilt or hesitation.

Affirmation & Gratitude

I embrace gratitude for joy, love, and creativity, allowing playful energy to renew and uplift my heart today.

Scorpio
19 April 2026

Scorpio, the Sun shifts into Taurus, bringing relationships into sharp focus. Partnerships—romantic, professional, or friendships—become highlighted. Conversations may bring clarity, offering opportunities to deepen bonds or reset boundaries. Passion feels strong, but patience ensures longevity. Saturn reminds you that real intimacy grows through respect and consistency. For singles, attraction may feel magnetic, but alignment matters more than chemistry. This is a day to strengthen love through balance and empathy.

Affirmation & Gratitude

I give thanks for love and connection, embracing patience, honesty, and respect to nurture meaningful and lasting relationships today.

Scorpio
20 April 2026

Scorpio, career and reputation come into focus. Recognition may arise, or opportunities could present themselves. Step into visibility with confidence—your depth stands out. Avoid chasing validation; instead, align your ambition with purpose. Today is about showing leadership with humility. Authority figures or mentors may provide guidance or acknowledgment. The cosmos reminds you that your career isn't just about achievement, but about embodying your true calling.

Affirmation & Gratitude

I am grateful for career opportunities, stepping forward with courage, authenticity, and purpose to create lasting success today.

Scorpio
21 April 2026

Scorpio, introspection is encouraged today. The Moon highlights your inner world, asking you to release what no longer serves you. Quiet reflection, journaling, or meditation will help uncover clarity. Pay attention to subtle signs—your intuition is especially sharp now. Rest is vital, not wasteful. Growth doesn't always require constant action—it often begins with silence. By honoring your need for stillness, you prepare for deeper transformation ahead.

Affirmation & Gratitude

I honor gratitude for rest and inner wisdom, trusting reflection and intuition to guide clarity, peace, and renewal.

Scorpio
22 April 2026

Scorpio, friendships and community bring inspiration today. Social ties or collaborations may spark fresh ideas for your future. The cosmos reminds you of the strength found in connection. Surround yourself with uplifting influences, and avoid those who drain energy. Someone in your circle may provide unexpected support or perspective. By aligning with community, your path broadens, and opportunities multiply. This is a day for shared growth and vision.

Affirmation & Gratitude

I am grateful for inspiring friendships, embracing collaboration and supportive networks that expand opportunity, creativity, and growth today.

Scorpio
23 April 2026

Scorpio, creativity and romance shine brightly. Venus enhances your magnetism, making you magnetic in relationships and expressive in art or passion projects. This is a powerful day for joyful expression—whether through love, hobbies, or playful activities. Don't dismiss fun as frivolous; it restores your spirit and attracts new inspiration. Your natural intensity softens when balanced with joy. Today, love and laughter are your healing tools. Celebrate them without guilt.

Affirmation & Gratitude

I embrace gratitude for joy, love, and creativity, allowing passion and playfulness to inspire and uplift my spirit today.

Scorpio
24 April 2026

Scorpio, routines and wellness need attention. The stars ask you to assess habits honestly—are they fueling your energy or draining it? Small adjustments today can bring long-term rewards. At work, focus on organization and structure; your efficiency will shine. Balance productivity with self-care to avoid burnout. Transformation grows through discipline and consistency, not force. This is your chance to ground yourself in practices that sustain success.

Affirmation & Gratitude

I am grateful for balance in my routines, creating healthy habits that nurture my wellbeing, clarity, and long-term growth.

Scorpio
25 April 2026

Scorpio, relationships take center stage. The Sun in Taurus illuminates your partnership zone, asking you to focus on balance and honesty. Conversations may bring breakthroughs or test patience, but both strengthen bonds when approached with openness. Passion is strong, but Saturn insists on responsibility alongside desire. If single, attraction may feel magnetic, yet alignment matters more than intensity. This is a day for authenticity in love, friendships, and professional connections.

Affirmation & Gratitude

I give thanks for love and connection, embracing honesty, patience, and respect to deepen relationships meaningfully today.

Scorpio
26 April 2026

Scorpio, career energy rises strongly today. Opportunities for recognition or advancement may arrive—step forward with confidence. Authority figures or mentors could notice your persistence. Success comes not from proving yourself, but from aligning ambition with authenticity. Be bold but stay humble. Today is about strengthening your reputation by showing resilience and purpose. The stars remind you that legacy grows when your work is aligned with your calling.

Affirmation & Gratitude

I am grateful for career opportunities, stepping forward with authenticity, courage, and integrity to create success that lasts.

Scorpio
27 April 2026

Scorpio, introspection brings renewal. The Moon encourages rest, healing, and reflection. Pay attention to dreams or synchronicities; they carry hidden messages. Avoid forcing outcomes—clarity comes through silence. This is a day for spiritual practices, journaling, or simply slowing down. Release outdated beliefs or fears holding you back. Growth often begins in the quiet moments when you realign with your inner truth. Trust the wisdom you uncover today.

Affirmation & Gratitude

I honor gratitude for rest and reflection, trusting stillness and intuition to restore clarity, healing, and strength today.

Scorpio
28 April 2026

Scorpio, friendships and community highlight your day. Social interactions, networking, or teamwork could bring fresh ideas. A friend's support or insight may shift your perspective. Collaboration amplifies success, but choose uplifting company—energy given to the wrong circles will drain you. Today's lesson: you don't need to walk alone. Supportive alliances broaden your opportunities and add strength to your vision. Value your role in your community—it matters more than you realize.

Affirmation & Gratitude

I am grateful for supportive friendships and shared vision, embracing collaboration that inspires creativity, growth, and opportunity today.

Scorpio
29 April 2026

Scorpio, creativity and joy take the lead again. The stars invite you to embrace playful energy, romance, or artistic pursuits. Venus enhances your magnetism—whether through love or creative expression, you're glowing. Don't hold back—joy is transformative, not trivial. Laughter, art, or passion restores your energy and opens new doors. Today is about celebrating life fully, not just enduring it. Allow yourself to shine with authenticity and vibrance.

Affirmation & Gratitude

I embrace gratitude for joy and passion, allowing love, creativity, and laughter to uplift and renew my heart today.

Scorpio
30 April 2026

Scorpio, routines and health are emphasized today. The stars ask you to take a closer look at your habits—are they supporting your goals or holding you back? Productivity feels strong, yet balance is essential. Organize, refine, and streamline your schedule to ease pressure. Focus on nourishment and self-care alongside responsibility. Transformation grows through sustainable effort, not overexertion. By grounding yourself in practical actions today, you prepare the way for greater progress ahead.

Affirmation & Gratitude

I am grateful for healthy routines and balance, choosing habits that nurture clarity, vitality, and long-term success today.

May
2026

Scorpio
01 May 2026

Scorpio, relationships come into focus as the month begins. The Sun highlights your partnership sector, urging patience, honesty, and balance in love and collaboration. Tensions may surface, but they're opportunities to deepen understanding. Passion is strong, yet Saturn insists on responsibility alongside desire. If single, attraction feels magnetic, but alignment matters more than chemistry. Today's conversations set the tone for how you approach connection this month—lead with empathy and openness.

Affirmation & Gratitude

I give thanks for meaningful connections, choosing honesty, empathy, and respect to nurture love and partnership today.

Scorpio
02 May 2026

Scorpio, career energy surges today. Recognition or new responsibilities may present themselves, and authority figures could notice your persistence. Step forward confidently, but with humility. Align ambition with purpose—success aligned with your authentic path will endure. Avoid comparing yourself to others; your journey is unique. This is a day to embody leadership with integrity, showing others the depth of your determination. Your influence grows when you stay true to yourself.

Affirmation & Gratitude

I am grateful for opportunities to grow in my career, embracing authenticity, courage, and purpose to build lasting success.

Scorpio
03 May 2026

Scorpio, the Moon draws you inward, urging rest and reflection. Emotions may feel heightened, but clarity comes when you slow down. Pay attention to dreams, inner nudges, or synchronicities—they're guiding you. This is a day to let go of what no longer supports you, clearing emotional clutter. Meditation, journaling, or creative solitude will bring renewal. Growth doesn't always require action—it often begins in silence and surrender. Trust the wisdom within.

Affirmation & Gratitude

I honor gratitude for rest and reflection, trusting inner guidance to restore clarity, peace, and renewal today.

Scorpio
04 May 2026

Scorpio, friendships and social circles inspire you today. Conversations, collaborations, or networking may spark new opportunities. A friend's encouragement could shift your perspective in a meaningful way. Choose uplifting company, and avoid draining dynamics. Today, teamwork amplifies success, reminding you that community matters in your growth. Invest energy where there's mutual support. By aligning with the right people, your vision expands, and opportunities open in ways you can't achieve alone.

Affirmation & Gratitude

I am grateful for supportive friendships, embracing collaboration that inspires creativity, shared growth, and meaningful opportunities today.

Scorpio
05 May 2026

Scorpio, creativity and joy flow abundantly. Venus enhances your magnetism, inspiring love, playfulness, and artistic expression. Relationships thrive when approached with lightness, not control. Passion runs high, but authenticity makes it meaningful. Hobbies, laughter, or artistic pursuits will uplift your spirit and fuel inspiration. Don't dismiss fun as trivial—it restores balance and renews your energy. Celebrate life unapologetically today. Your heart is strongest when joy fuels it.

Affirmation & Gratitude

I embrace gratitude for joy, love, and creativity, allowing passion and playfulness to inspire and renew my heart today.

Scorpio
06 May 2026

Scorpio, routines and health return to focus. The cosmos asks you to refine habits for balance. Work requires attention, but efficiency improves when you stay organized and mindful. Avoid overexertion—sustainable progress is key. Health matters also benefit from small improvements today. Remember, transformation doesn't always come from dramatic change, but from steady, consistent effort. Ground yourself in simple, practical actions. Today is about building stability and strength in both body and spirit.

Affirmation & Gratitude

I give thanks for balance in my daily life, creating routines that support clarity, wellbeing, and long-term growth.

Scorpio
07 May 2026

Scorpio, relationships take the spotlight today. The Sun in Taurus highlights your partnership zone, encouraging balance and patience. Conversations may feel intense, but breakthroughs are possible if honesty leads the way. Passion is present, yet Saturn insists on responsibility alongside desire. If single, magnetic attraction may spark, but discernment is key. Today asks you to choose authenticity over control, nurturing connections that feel stable and true.

Affirmation & Gratitude

I give thanks for meaningful partnerships, embracing honesty, patience, and respect to deepen love and build authentic connections today.

Scorpio
08 May 2026

Scorpio, career energy strengthens under today's alignment. Recognition may arrive, or an authority figure could acknowledge your persistence. Step forward with confidence but avoid arrogance. Success comes from aligning ambition with authenticity. The cosmos reminds you to focus not just on achievement, but on the legacy you're building. Today's opportunities may shape your long-term path, so stay mindful of your choices.

Affirmation & Gratitude

I am grateful for career growth, stepping into visibility with courage, authenticity, and alignment to purpose today.

Scorpio
09 May 2026

Scorpio, introspection is emphasized. The Moon highlights your spiritual sector, urging you to slow down, rest, and reconnect with intuition. Dreams and synchronicities carry guidance—pay attention. This is not a day for pushing outward, but for inner clarity and release. Quiet practices, like journaling or meditation, refresh your spirit. Growth often begins in silence, and today offers space for renewal. Trust your inner compass.

Affirmation & Gratitude

I honor gratitude for stillness and reflection, trusting my intuition to guide clarity, peace, and renewal today.

Scorpio
10 May 2026

Scorpio, friendships and social networks bring inspiration. Group activities, collaborations, or conversations may spark ideas that expand your vision. Choose uplifting company—your energy is valuable. A friend's perspective could reveal new possibilities. Today reminds you of the power of connection and teamwork. By sharing your vision, you attract allies who align with your path. Supportive community strengthens your confidence and opens new opportunities.

Affirmation & Gratitude

I am grateful for supportive friendships, embracing collaboration and community that inspire growth, creativity, and opportunity today.

Scorpio
11 May 2026

Scorpio, joy and creativity thrive. Venus enhances your playful side, inviting romance, laughter, and artistic expression. Love feels magnetic, and passion flows freely, but authenticity gives it depth. Allow yourself to celebrate beauty, hobbies, or fun without guilt. Joy is transformative, reminding you that balance comes through lightheartedness as much as intensity. Today is about embracing what makes your spirit feel alive and vibrant.

Affirmation & Gratitude

I embrace gratitude for love, joy, and creativity, allowing passion and playfulness to inspire and renew my heart today.

Scorpio
12 May 2026

Scorpio, health and routines require focus today. The stars urge you to refine habits for better balance. Small changes, like rest, hydration, or organization, have long-term benefits. At work, efficiency is your strength, but avoid perfectionism. Sustainable progress matters more than speed. Today is about building stability through consistent, intentional practices that nurture both body and spirit. Transformation grows from small, daily steps.

Affirmation & Gratitude

I give thanks for balance in my routines, choosing habits that support clarity, wellbeing, and long-term growth today.

Scorpio
13 May 2026

Scorpio, relationships are highlighted again. Conversations may feel deep or revealing, offering chances to reset balance or strengthen trust. Passion is present, yet maturity matters more than intensity. Single Scorpios may feel drawn toward magnetic attraction, but clarity comes with time. Today reminds you that authentic love is built through respect, honesty, and patience. Lean into openness—true intimacy grows when both hearts remain vulnerable and real.

Affirmation & Gratitude

I am grateful for love and connection, embracing honesty, respect, and patience to nurture meaningful relationships today.

Scorpio
14 May 2026

Scorpio, career energy builds again. The stars highlight recognition and responsibility, showing that your persistence is paying off. Opportunities may arise through mentors or authority figures. Step forward with authenticity, not ego—your depth already distinguishes you. Today is about aligning ambition with your greater calling. Avoid comparing your path to others; your journey is unique. Focus on building something lasting and purposeful.

Affirmation & Gratitude

I give thanks for career recognition, embracing authenticity, courage, and humility to create meaningful, lasting success today.

Scorpio
15 May 2026

Scorpio, introspection takes the lead. The Moon pulls you inward, asking you to rest, reflect, and release. Pay attention to subtle signs—dreams, synchronicities, or feelings guide your choices. Avoid forcing progress; clarity comes in stillness. This is a day for spiritual renewal, journaling, or quiet contemplation. Growth begins beneath the surface, and today offers space to recalibrate. Trust your intuition—it's sharper than ever now.

Affirmation & Gratitude

I honor gratitude for rest and stillness, trusting intuition to guide me toward clarity, healing, and renewal today.

Scorpio
16 May 2026

Scorpio, friendships and social connections energize you. Collaborations or group activities may spark fresh inspiration. A friend's perspective could open new opportunities. Choose uplifting company—your time is too precious for draining dynamics. Community helps expand your vision and adds momentum to your goals. Today's energy reminds you that growth is multiplied when shared. Surround yourself with people who respect your depth and align with your path.

Affirmation & Gratitude

I am grateful for supportive friendships and community, embracing collaboration that inspires creativity, opportunity, and shared growth today.

Scorpio
17 May 2026

Scorpio, creativity and love flow abundantly. Venus highlights your magnetism, making today perfect for romance, passion projects, or playful activities. Joy restores balance, reminding you that lighthearted energy is just as transformative as intensity. Engage in hobbies or artistic expression to ignite inspiration. Relationships thrive when you lean into laughter and presence. Don't underestimate the healing power of fun—it lifts your spirit and opens doors.

Affirmation & Gratitude

I embrace gratitude for joy, love, and creativity, allowing playful energy to uplift and renew my heart today.

Scorpio
18 May 2026

Scorpio, the focus shifts to health and routines. Work requires attention, but sustainable progress is more important than speed. Refine your habits—nourishment, rest, and organization support clarity. Transformation begins with consistent daily steps, not drastic changes. Balance productivity with self-care; both are essential for long-term growth. Today is about grounding yourself in practices that fuel your energy and strengthen resilience.

Affirmation & Gratitude

I give thanks for healthy routines and balance, choosing habits that nurture wellbeing, clarity, and sustainable success today.

Scorpio
19 May 2026

Scorpio, relationships come into sharp focus. Conversations may feel revealing, offering chances to deepen intimacy or reset boundaries. Passion is strong, but maturity matters most. For singles, attraction feels magnetic, but alignment reveals itself over time. The cosmos asks you to prioritize honesty and patience in all bonds. True intimacy grows from vulnerability, respect, and balance. Today offers lessons in building love that lasts.

Affirmation & Gratitude

I am grateful for meaningful relationships, embracing honesty, patience, and respect to nurture love and authentic connection today.

Scorpio
20 May 2026

Scorpio, the Sun enters Gemini, shifting your focus to transformation and deeper truths. Emotional layers surface, asking you to explore what lies beneath. This is a time for releasing fears, debts, or attachments that no longer serve you. Conversations around shared resources or intimacy may arise. The cosmos encourages you to embrace honesty with yourself and others. Growth comes from facing truths and allowing transformation to unfold.

Affirmation & Gratitude

I give thanks for transformation, courageously releasing what no longer serves me and embracing renewal with authenticity and strength today.

Scorpio
21 May 2026

Scorpio, today's energy highlights shared resources and transformation. The Sun in Gemini illuminates areas where you merge finances, emotions, or responsibilities with others. Conversations may bring clarity about money, trust, or intimacy. The stars encourage you to be transparent, even if difficult truths arise. This is a powerful time to release unhealthy attachments and step into empowerment. Transformation grows when you claim your worth without apology.

Affirmation & Gratitude

I am grateful for clarity in shared matters, embracing honesty and empowerment to create balance, stability, and trust today.

Scorpio
22 May 2026

Scorpio, introspection deepens under today's Moon. Emotions may rise unexpectedly, asking for your attention. Rather than resist, lean into reflection. Healing happens when you acknowledge rather than suppress. Journaling or meditation can uncover insights that transform how you see yourself and your path. Release lingering fears—growth requires space for renewal. The cosmos reminds you: your strength is not diminished by vulnerability; it's amplified by it.

Affirmation & Gratitude

I honor gratitude for self-reflection and healing, trusting vulnerability to reveal clarity, strength, and transformation today.

Scorpio
23 May 2026

Scorpio, friendships and community connections are energized. Conversations or group activities could spark fresh ideas for your future. Surround yourself with uplifting people who encourage your growth. A friend's support may shift your perspective, helping you see possibilities you hadn't considered. Collaboration is highlighted—shared vision creates momentum. By engaging with community, you strengthen not only your own path but also the collective energy. Choose alliances that align with your values.

Affirmation & Gratitude

I am grateful for supportive friendships and shared vision, embracing collaboration that inspires creativity, opportunity, and growth today.

Scorpio
24 May 2026

Scorpio, romance and creativity flourish today. Venus enhances your magnetism, attracting attention in love and fueling artistic pursuits. Passion feels strong, but authenticity matters most. Relationships thrive when you approach them with joy and playfulness. Creative breakthroughs may also come easily—trust your inspiration. Fun isn't trivial; it recharges your spirit and draws new opportunities. Today is about celebrating what makes your heart beat faster. Lean into joy—it transforms everything.

Affirmation & Gratitude

I embrace gratitude for joy, passion, and creativity, allowing love and inspiration to uplift and renew my spirit today.

Scorpio
25 May 2026

Scorpio, routines and responsibilities call for attention. The cosmos asks you to refine habits—small adjustments create long-term stability. Work requires focus, but don't sacrifice self-care. Balance productivity with rest, and your efficiency will soar. Today is about aligning effort with wellbeing. Discipline is your ally, not a burden. Transformation comes from consistent, intentional actions that nurture your body, mind, and goals. Trust steady steps—they build lasting change.

Affirmation & Gratitude

I give thanks for balance and structure, creating daily habits that nurture clarity, vitality, and sustainable progress today.

Scorpio
26 May 2026

Scorpio, relationships move into focus again. Conversations may reveal truths that shift dynamics, offering chances to deepen intimacy or reset boundaries. Passion is heightened, but patience ensures stability. Single Scorpios may encounter magnetic attraction, though alignment reveals itself in time. Today's energy teaches that honesty and openness strengthen all bonds—romantic, platonic, or professional. By embracing authenticity, you create space for love to grow naturally.

Affirmation & Gratitude

I am grateful for meaningful connections, choosing honesty, patience, and empathy to nurture deeper, authentic relationships today.

Scorpio
27 May 2026

Scorpio, career matters intensify. Recognition may arise, or new responsibilities could expand your influence. Step forward confidently—your persistence is paying off. Authority figures or mentors may notice your efforts, opening doors for advancement. Today's energy asks you to align ambition with your higher calling. Success is not only achievement—it's purpose in action. Stay grounded in integrity, and your reputation will flourish.

Affirmation & Gratitude

I am grateful for career opportunities, embracing authenticity, courage, and integrity to build meaningful and lasting success today.

Scorpio
28 May 2026

Scorpio, the Moon draws you inward, inviting reflection and renewal. Emotions may feel close to the surface, but they carry wisdom. Pay attention to dreams, subtle signs, or intuitive nudges—they're guiding you toward clarity. Avoid pushing forward; today is best for spiritual practices or quiet rest. Release what feels heavy and unnecessary. By embracing stillness, you prepare space for transformation and regain balance. Growth often begins in silence.

Affirmation & Gratitude

I honor gratitude for rest and stillness, trusting my intuition to guide renewal, peace, and clarity today.

Scorpio
29 May 2026

Scorpio, friendships and community highlight your day. Group activities or conversations may spark exciting ideas. Surround yourself with supportive people who encourage growth. A friend's perspective could shift how you view a situation. Collaboration brings momentum, but discern where to place your energy. The cosmos reminds you: shared vision multiplies success. Invest time where mutual respect thrives, and you'll strengthen both your path and your community.

Affirmation & Gratitude

I am grateful for supportive friendships and collaborations, embracing shared vision that inspires creativity, opportunity, and growth today.

Scorpio
30 May 2026

Scorpio, joy and creativity thrive. Venus enhances your magnetism, inspiring romance, laughter, and artistic pursuits. Passion flows strongly, but authenticity makes it meaningful. Don't dismiss fun—it restores balance and recharges your spirit. Children, play, or hobbies may bring fresh inspiration. Relationships deepen when you share lighthearted moments as much as serious ones. Today is about celebrating beauty and love unapologetically. Allow yourself to shine with joy—it attracts blessings.

Affirmation & Gratitude

I embrace gratitude for love, creativity, and joy, allowing passion and playfulness to uplift and renew my spirit today.

Scorpio
31 May 2026

Scorpio, wellness and structure require attention. The cosmos asks you to refine routines, focusing on balance between work and rest. Productivity flows best when paired with care for your body and mind. Small improvements—better organization, rest, or nourishment—yield long-lasting results. Discipline is your ally today, not a burden. By grounding yourself in consistent practices, you strengthen clarity and resilience for the future. Transformation builds step by step.

Affirmation & Gratitude

I give thanks for balance in routines, creating habits that nurture health, clarity, and stability today.

June
2026

Scorpio
01 June 2026

Scorpio, relationships are in focus. The Sun highlights your partnership zone, encouraging balance, patience, and respect. Conversations may feel revealing, offering chances to reset or deepen bonds. Passion is heightened, but Saturn insists on responsibility alongside desire. If single, attraction may feel magnetic, yet time will reveal alignment. Today, authentic love is built through honesty and empathy.

Affirmation & Gratitude

I am grateful for meaningful connections, choosing honesty, patience, and respect to nurture deeper relationships today.

Scorpio
02 June 2026

Scorpio, career momentum strengthens. Recognition or opportunity may arise, bringing validation for your persistence. Authority figures may notice your efforts. Step into visibility with authenticity and confidence—success aligned with your purpose lasts. The cosmos asks you to align ambition with integrity. Today is about leading by example, not comparison. By owning your strength gracefully, you open doors for long-term advancement.

Affirmation & Gratitude

I am grateful for career opportunities, embracing courage, authenticity, and purpose to create meaningful success today.

Scorpio
03 June 2026

Scorpio, the cosmos highlights your inner world, urging reflection and release. Emotional depth feels strong, but this is clarity, not burden. Pay attention to dreams, intuition, and symbols—they hold guidance. Avoid pushing forward; today is about healing. Rest restores strength for the next cycle. Growth often begins with letting go of what no longer serves you. Surrender creates space for transformation to emerge naturally.

Affirmation & Gratitude

I honor gratitude for stillness and reflection, trusting my inner wisdom to guide clarity, renewal, and strength today.

Scorpio
04 June 2026

Scorpio, friendships and community highlight your day. The stars encourage collaboration—shared projects or group conversations may spark inspiration. A friend's encouragement could provide clarity or open doors to opportunity. Surround yourself with uplifting people who respect your depth. Today reminds you that your growth is amplified when aligned with supportive connections. Choose carefully where to invest energy—your time is precious. Community is your catalyst for expansion.

Affirmation & Gratitude

I am grateful for inspiring friendships, embracing collaboration and shared vision that expand creativity, growth, and opportunity today.

Scorpio
05 June 2026

Scorpio, creativity and love flow freely. Venus amplifies your charm, making this an excellent day for romance, artistic pursuits, or playful expression. Passion runs high, but presence matters more than intensity. Don't underestimate the healing power of joy—it restores balance and energizes your spirit. Allow yourself to lean into laughter, beauty, and inspiration. Today is about celebrating life unapologetically, honoring what makes you feel alive and radiant.

Affirmation & Gratitude

I embrace gratitude for joy, love, and creativity, allowing passion and playfulness to uplift and inspire my heart today.

Scorpio
06 June 2026

Scorpio, wellness and structure demand focus. The Moon highlights routines, encouraging you to refine habits. Small adjustments today strengthen clarity and resilience. Productivity flows best when balanced with nourishment and rest. Transformation is built through consistency, not extremes. Organize your schedule, simplify tasks, and prioritize self-care. Today is about creating a rhythm that sustains growth long term.

Affirmation & Gratitude

I give thanks for balance in my daily routines, creating habits that nurture clarity, vitality, and stability today.

Scorpio
07 June 2026

Scorpio, relationships come into focus. The Sun highlights your partnership zone, encouraging deeper honesty and patience. Tension may arise, but breakthroughs come with openness. Passion is strong, but maturity matters most. If single, attraction feels magnetic, but true alignment reveals itself with time. In all connections, vulnerability and respect build lasting love. The cosmos reminds you: intimacy thrives on authenticity.

Affirmation & Gratitude

I am grateful for meaningful connections, choosing honesty, patience, and empathy to nurture love and authentic relationships today.

Scorpio
08 June 2026

Scorpio, career matters take center stage. Recognition or responsibility may arise, spotlighting your resilience. Authority figures could notice your efforts, opening doors for advancement. Align ambition with integrity—success is most enduring when authentic. Avoid comparing your progress with others; your journey is unique. Today is about stepping forward confidently and allowing your determination to speak for itself. Your influence grows when rooted in purpose.

Affirmation & Gratitude

I am grateful for career opportunities, embracing courage, authenticity, and purpose to create lasting success today.

Scorpio
09 June 2026

Scorpio, introspection brings clarity. The Moon draws you inward, urging rest and reflection. Dreams and synchronicities may deliver insight —listen closely. Avoid pushing outward; today is best for spiritual renewal and emotional release. Quiet practices like journaling or meditation restore your strength. Transformation often begins in silence, and today offers space to prepare for new beginnings. Trust your intuition—it's speaking clearly.

Affirmation & Gratitude

I honor gratitude for stillness and reflection, trusting inner wisdom to guide renewal, clarity, and peace today.

Scorpio
10 June 2026

Scorpio, friendships and community energize you. Conversations, collaborations, or group activities may spark new ideas or opportunities. Choose circles that uplift and support your growth. A friend's advice could reveal solutions to a lingering challenge. The cosmos reminds you: teamwork multiplies your vision, but discernment protects your energy. Today, community strengthens your path and amplifies your impact.

Affirmation & Gratitude

I am grateful for supportive friendships and collaborations, embracing shared vision that inspires creativity, opportunity, and growth today.

Scorpio
11 June 2026

Scorpio, creativity and romance are lit up today. Venus amplifies your magnetism, making this a perfect day for love, joy, and self-expression. Passion flows easily, but authenticity keeps it meaningful. Hobbies or artistic projects may bring breakthroughs. Fun isn't frivolous—it renews your energy and restores balance. The stars remind you that laughter and beauty are just as transformative as intensity. Lean into joy without hesitation.

Affirmation & Gratitude

I embrace gratitude for love, joy, and creativity, allowing playfulness and passion to uplift and renew my spirit today.

Scorpio
12 June 2026

Scorpio, focus shifts to routines and health. The cosmos urges you to refine your habits—small, steady steps create lasting change. Work requires attention, but don't sacrifice rest or nourishment. Transformation is not about extremes; it's about balance. By aligning your daily rhythm with care and discipline, you create stability and clarity. This is a day to prioritize self-care alongside responsibility, ensuring sustainable energy for the weeks ahead.

Affirmation & Gratitude

I am grateful for balance in my daily life, creating habits that nurture clarity, health, and long-term strength today.

Scorpio
13 June 2026

Scorpio, relationships come into the spotlight. The Sun highlights your partnership zone, encouraging openness and patience. Conversations may reveal truths that deepen trust or reset boundaries. Passion is present, but Saturn reminds you that maturity builds stability. If single, attraction feels magnetic, but clarity comes with time. Today asks you to lead with empathy rather than control, nurturing bonds through honesty and respect.

Affirmation & Gratitude

I give thanks for meaningful connections, choosing honesty, patience, and respect to deepen love and authentic relationships today.

Scorpio
14 June 2026

Scorpio, career momentum builds. Recognition or responsibility may come your way, highlighting your resilience. Authority figures may acknowledge your efforts, opening doors for future success. Align ambition with authenticity—success rooted in integrity lasts longer. Avoid chasing approval; focus instead on purpose. Today is about showing leadership through depth, determination, and humility. When you embody your calling, opportunities naturally follow.

Affirmation & Gratitude

I am grateful for career opportunities, stepping forward with courage, authenticity, and integrity to build meaningful success today.

Scorpio
15 June 2026

Scorpio, introspection brings clarity today. The Moon urges you to step back, rest, and listen within. Emotional sensitivity may rise, but it's guiding you. Dreams, symbols, or inner whispers carry messages for your path. Avoid forcing outcomes—this is a day for healing and quiet renewal. Transformation begins in stillness. By honoring your inner world, you align with your deeper strength and wisdom.

Affirmation & Gratitude

I honor gratitude for stillness and reflection, trusting intuition to bring clarity, peace, and renewal today.

Scorpio
16 June 2026

Scorpio, friendships and community bring energy. Conversations or collaborations may inspire new opportunities. A friend's perspective could help you see possibilities differently. Invest your energy where mutual respect thrives. Today, teamwork is a catalyst, amplifying your vision and momentum. The cosmos reminds you that community doesn't weaken independence—it strengthens it. Supportive alliances expand your path and fuel your growth.

Affirmation & Gratitude

I am grateful for supportive friendships and shared vision, embracing collaboration that inspires growth, creativity, and opportunity today.

Scorpio
17 June 2026

Scorpio, creativity and joy flow abundantly. Venus enhances your magnetism, making today excellent for romance, artistic pursuits, or simply celebrating life. Passion is strong, but playfulness makes it meaningful. Hobbies, fun, and laughter restore balance and open your spirit to inspiration. Love deepens when you share joy as much as intensity. Today's cosmic message is simple—choose joy unapologetically, and allow it to transform your path forward.

Affirmation & Gratitude

I embrace gratitude for joy, love, and creativity, allowing passion and play to uplift and renew my spirit today.

Scorpio
18 June 2026

Scorpio, today emphasizes wellness and discipline. The Moon highlights your routines, urging you to refine habits that sustain energy. Work feels demanding, but efficiency grows when paired with balance. Avoid overexertion—steady progress outlasts extremes. Nourishment, rest, and order support clarity. By grounding yourself in practical steps, you prepare for future breakthroughs. Transformation begins with daily rhythm, not dramatic leaps.

Affirmation & Gratitude

I am grateful for balance in my routines, creating habits that nurture health, clarity, and long-term strength today.

Scorpio
19 June 2026

Scorpio, relationships come into focus. The Sun in Gemini highlights intimacy, shared resources, and deeper emotional bonds. Conversations may reveal truths, helping you reset boundaries or strengthen trust. Passion is present, but respect and patience ensure stability. Single Scorpios may feel magnetic attraction, but alignment matters more than intensity. Today teaches that intimacy deepens through honesty and openness.

Affirmation & Gratitude

I give thanks for love and connection, embracing honesty, patience, and respect to nurture deeper, authentic relationships today.

Scorpio
20 June 2026

Scorpio, career matters intensify. Recognition or new responsibilities could place you in the spotlight. Authority figures may acknowledge your efforts, opening doors for advancement. Success is strongest when aligned with authenticity—don't chase validation. Today is about leadership grounded in purpose. Your resilience shines through perseverance, and others notice. Step forward with confidence, but remain humble.

Affirmation & Gratitude

I am grateful for opportunities in my career, stepping into visibility with courage, authenticity, and integrity to build meaningful success today.

Scorpio
21 June 2026

Scorpio, introspection is highlighted. The Moon draws you inward, urging rest, renewal, and reflection. Dreams and subtle signs may hold guidance for your path. Avoid rushing or forcing outcomes—clarity comes through silence. Journaling, meditation, or time in nature restores peace. Growth begins within, and today offers space to prepare for transformation. Trust your inner wisdom—it speaks clearly now.

Affirmation & Gratitude

I honor gratitude for stillness and reflection, trusting intuition to reveal clarity, healing, and renewal today.

Scorpio
22 June 2026

Scorpio, friendships and community energize you. Social ties or collaborations may spark new opportunities. A friend's support could shift your perspective and reveal hidden potential. Today is about amplifying your vision through teamwork, but choose wisely where to invest your energy. Uplifting alliances fuel your growth; draining ones hold you back. Surround yourself with those who celebrate your strength.

Affirmation & Gratitude

I am grateful for supportive friendships and shared vision, embracing collaboration that inspires growth, creativity, and opportunity today.

Scorpio
23 June 2026

Scorpio, creativity and joy flourish. Venus enhances your magnetism, inspiring romance, artistic pursuits, and playful energy. Passion runs high, but authenticity gives it depth. Love deepens when paired with laughter and lightheartedness. Fun is transformative—it restores balance and draws blessings. Today is about celebrating beauty and expressing yourself freely. Creativity and joy are not luxuries—they're catalysts for renewal.

Affirmation & Gratitude

I embrace gratitude for love, joy, and creativity, allowing passion and playfulness to uplift and inspire my spirit today.

Scorpio
24 June 2026

Scorpio, health and structure are emphasized again. The cosmos urges you to refine habits and focus on sustainable growth. Work requires focus, but don't neglect rest or nourishment. Transformation happens through consistent, practical choices. Small improvements in diet, organization, or discipline create long-term benefits. Today is about building stability through steady action. Balance ensures both productivity and peace.

Affirmation & Gratitude

I give thanks for balance in daily life, creating routines that nurture clarity, wellbeing, and long-term strength today.

Scorpio
25 June 2026

Scorpio, relationships dominate the day. The Sun and Moon emphasize intimacy, asking you to examine balance in love, trust, and shared resources. Conversations may reveal hidden truths, but don't shy away—clarity strengthens bonds. Passion is heightened, yet stability requires patience. If single, magnetic attraction may appear, but discernment matters most. Authenticity deepens all bonds today.

Affirmation & Gratitude

I give thanks for love and connection, choosing honesty, patience, and respect to nurture meaningful and lasting relationships today.

Scorpio
26 June 2026

Scorpio, career and public life gain momentum. Recognition or new responsibilities may put you in the spotlight. Authority figures could notice your dedication. Step forward with confidence—your persistence shines. Today is about aligning ambition with authenticity; success built on truth lasts longest. Leadership comes naturally now, so embrace opportunities. Remember, your purpose isn't just achievement—it's legacy.

Affirmation & Gratitude

I am grateful for career opportunities, stepping forward with authenticity, courage, and purpose to create meaningful and lasting success today.

Scorpio
27 June 2026

Scorpio, introspection calls. The Moon activates your spiritual zone, urging you to rest, reflect, and reconnect with your inner wisdom. Emotional sensitivity is high, but clarity emerges when you embrace silence. Avoid overextending outwardly—today is for renewal. Journaling, meditation, or solitude reveals truths you've overlooked. Transformation begins within, and today creates space for growth.

Affirmation & Gratitude

I honor gratitude for stillness and reflection, trusting intuition to reveal clarity, healing, and renewal today.

Scorpio
28 June 2026

Scorpio, friendships and community energize you. Social gatherings, collaborations, or group projects may spark fresh opportunities. A friend's insight could shift your perspective, helping you see potential in new ways. Surround yourself with uplifting people who share your vision. Community strengthens your confidence and expands your reach. Choose alliances wisely—your time is precious.

Affirmation & Gratitude

I am grateful for supportive friendships and shared vision, embracing collaboration that inspires creativity, opportunity, and growth today.

Scorpio
29 June 2026

Scorpio, creativity and joy are highlighted today. Venus enhances your magnetism, making this a perfect time for romance, art, or playful expression. Love feels deeper when paired with laughter and lightheartedness. Creative breakthroughs are possible if you allow inspiration to flow naturally. Fun is transformative—it restores balance and attracts blessings. The stars remind you to celebrate life without guilt, honoring beauty and joy as much as intensity.

Affirmation & Gratitude

I embrace gratitude for joy, passion, and creativity, allowing playful energy to inspire, uplift, and renew my spirit today.

Scorpio
30 June 2026

Scorpio, wellness and daily rhythm need attention. The Moon emphasizes structure, urging you to refine routines that support balance. Work demands efficiency, but don't neglect rest or nourishment. Sustainable progress grows from small, steady steps. Avoid perfectionism; consistency creates lasting transformation. By grounding yourself in mindful habits, you strengthen clarity and resilience. Today is about aligning responsibilities with self-care for true growth.

Affirmation & Gratitude

I give thanks for balance in my routines, creating healthy habits that support clarity, vitality, and long-term wellbeing today.

July
2026

Scorpio
01 July 2026

Scorpio, relationships take focus. The Sun highlights your partnership zone, bringing opportunities for honesty and balance. Conversations may reveal truths that reshape dynamics. Passion feels strong, but Saturn insists maturity and respect must guide connections. If single, attraction may feel magnetic, but patience reveals alignment. Today reminds you that love deepens when authenticity leads.

Affirmation & Gratitude

I am grateful for love and connection, choosing honesty, patience, and respect to nurture authentic and meaningful relationships today.

Scorpio
02 July 2026

Scorpio, career energy strengthens. Recognition or new responsibilities may surface, drawing attention to your persistence. Authority figures may open doors of opportunity. Step forward with confidence—success aligned with authenticity lasts. Avoid comparing yourself to others; your path is unique. Today, your resilience and determination speak louder than words. Show leadership through integrity, and others will follow your example.

Affirmation & Gratitude

I am grateful for career opportunities, embracing courage, authenticity, and integrity to create meaningful success today.

Scorpio
03 July 2026

Scorpio, the Moon pulls you inward, emphasizing rest and renewal. Emotions may surface, but they carry insight. Reflection reveals truths you've overlooked. Spiritual practices, journaling, or meditation bring clarity. Avoid rushing; today is for healing, not action. Growth often begins in stillness. By honoring your inner world, you prepare space for transformation. Trust your intuition—it speaks loudly now.

Affirmation & Gratitude

I honor gratitude for stillness and reflection, trusting inner wisdom to guide me toward clarity, peace, and renewal today.

Scorpio
04 July 2026

Scorpio, friendships and community bring energy. Conversations or group activities may spark inspiration for your future. A friend's encouragement could help you see new opportunities. Collaboration expands your vision—shared goals amplify growth. Choose your company carefully; invest only where there's mutual respect and alignment. Today reminds you: community is a catalyst for progress.

Affirmation & Gratitude

I am grateful for supportive friendships and shared vision, embracing collaboration that inspires creativity, opportunity, and growth today.

Scorpio
05 July 2026

Scorpio, creativity and romance thrive today. Venus amplifies your charm, making you magnetic in love and expressive in art. Passion feels strong, but joy makes it meaningful. Don't dismiss fun—it's healing. Creative projects flow easily; inspiration surrounds you. Relationships deepen when shared with lightness. Today's cosmic message is simple: celebrate beauty, laughter, and love unapologetically. Joy is as transformative as intensity.

Affirmation & Gratitude

I embrace gratitude for love, joy, and creativity, allowing passion and playfulness to uplift and inspire my spirit today.

Scorpio
06 July 2026

Scorpio, wellness and routines require focus. The Moon emphasizes discipline, urging you to refine habits for balance. Work tasks feel heavy, but efficiency grows when paired with rest and nourishment. Sustainable progress is more powerful than quick fixes. Today is about grounding yourself in practices that nurture strength. Transformation begins with daily choices—keep them aligned with your wellbeing.

Affirmation & Gratitude

I am grateful for balance in my routines, creating habits that support clarity, energy, and long-term growth today.

Scorpio
07 July 2026

Scorpio, partnerships are highlighted. The Sun emphasizes honesty and balance in love and close ties. Tension may arise, but breakthroughs come with patience. Passion runs deep, yet Saturn reminds you that respect and maturity sustain relationships. If single, attraction feels magnetic, but discernment matters most. Authentic love grows through vulnerability and truth.

Affirmation & Gratitude

I give thanks for meaningful relationships, choosing honesty, patience, and respect to deepen love and connection today.

Scorpio
08 July 2026

Scorpio, career opportunities may surface today. Recognition, advancement, or new responsibilities highlight your persistence. Authority figures may take notice of your resilience. Step into visibility confidently, but remain grounded in integrity. The stars remind you: success aligned with purpose lasts longest. Today is about showing leadership authentically and embracing the influence you've earned through dedication.

Affirmation & Gratitude

I am grateful for career opportunities, stepping forward with courage, authenticity, and purpose to create lasting success today.

Scorpio
09 July 2026

Scorpio, introspection calls. The Moon draws you inward, asking for reflection and release. Emotions may rise, but they reveal truths you've avoided. Journaling, meditation, or solitude help you process and heal. Today is less about outward action and more about restoring balance. Growth begins in silence. Trust your inner guidance—it's pointing you toward renewal.

Affirmation & Gratitude

I honor gratitude for stillness and reflection, trusting inner wisdom to bring clarity, healing, and renewal today.

Scorpio
10 July 2026

Scorpio, friendships and social circles bring inspiration. Conversations may spark ideas that expand your vision. A friend's encouragement could shift your outlook positively. Collaboration amplifies growth, but choose uplifting alliances. Avoid those who drain your energy. Today is about recognizing the value of supportive community in your journey forward. Shared vision builds momentum.

Affirmation & Gratitude

I am grateful for supportive friendships and shared vision, embracing collaboration that inspires creativity, growth, and opportunity today.

Scorpio
11 July 2026

Scorpio, creativity and romance flourish. Venus highlights your magnetism, drawing love and artistic inspiration your way. Passion feels strong, but joy brings balance. Hobbies, laughter, or playful connections restore your energy. Creative breakthroughs are possible if you lean into inspiration. Today's cosmic reminder: joy is transformative, not frivolous. Celebrate beauty and love fully.

Affirmation & Gratitude

I embrace gratitude for joy, creativity, and love, allowing passion and play to uplift and inspire my spirit today.

Scorpio
12 July 2026

Scorpio, wellness and discipline return to focus. The cosmos urges you to refine your daily rhythm. Productivity thrives when balanced with rest and self-care. Sustainable success grows through consistent effort, not extremes. Focus on nourishment, organization, and grounding practices. Today is about building stability in both body and mind, ensuring strength for future progress.

Affirmation & Gratitude

I give thanks for balance in my routines, creating habits that nurture clarity, wellbeing, and long-term success today.

Scorpio
13 July 2026

Scorpio, relationships are highlighted today. The Sun emphasizes your partnership zone, asking you to bring balance, patience, and honesty into connections. Passion runs deep, but Saturn reminds you that respect and maturity form the foundation of lasting bonds. Single Scorpios may feel powerful attraction, but discernment is key. Today's cosmic lesson: intimacy grows when authenticity leads.

Affirmation & Gratitude

I am grateful for meaningful connections, choosing honesty, patience, and respect to nurture love and authentic relationships today.

Scorpio
14 July 2026

Scorpio, career matters take focus. Recognition may come your way, or new responsibilities may expand your influence. Authority figures could acknowledge your persistence. Step forward confidently, but ground yourself in integrity. The stars encourage ambition, but only when aligned with purpose. Today asks you to own your resilience and lead authentically. Success built on truth is lasting.

Affirmation & Gratitude

I give thanks for opportunities in my career, embracing authenticity, courage, and integrity to build meaningful success today.

Scorpio
15 July 2026

Scorpio, introspection is emphasized. The Moon highlights your inner world, encouraging rest and reflection. Emotional sensitivity is heightened—listen carefully to what surfaces. Dreams, synchronicities, or subtle nudges may provide answers. Avoid pushing outwardly; today is best for spiritual renewal and emotional release. Transformation begins when you make space for healing. Trust your intuition—it knows the way.

Affirmation & Gratitude

I honor gratitude for stillness and reflection, trusting intuition to guide clarity, renewal, and peace today.

Scorpio
16 July 2026

Scorpio, friendships and community connections energize you. Conversations or group projects may spark fresh opportunities. A friend's perspective could inspire new paths forward. Collaboration brings momentum, but discernment is key. Choose uplifting allies and avoid those who drain energy. Today's cosmic reminder: your vision expands when shared with the right people. Community is your strength.

Affirmation & Gratitude

I am grateful for supportive friendships and shared vision, embracing collaboration that inspires growth, creativity, and opportunity today.

Scorpio
17 July 2026

Scorpio, creativity and romance flourish today. Venus enhances your magnetism, drawing love and artistic inspiration your way. Passion runs strong, but joy deepens its meaning. Explore hobbies, playful energy, or expressive outlets. Relationships thrive when laughter joins intensity. The cosmos reminds you that joy isn't trivial—it's transformative. Today, celebrate beauty, love, and creativity without holding back.

Affirmation & Gratitude

I embrace gratitude for love, joy, and creativity, allowing passion and playfulness to uplift and inspire my spirit today.

Scorpio
18 July 2026

Scorpio, wellness and routines require attention. The stars urge you to refine your daily habits. Small adjustments—better rest, nourishment, or organization—bring long-term results. Productivity grows when paired with balance, not overexertion. Today's lesson is that transformation comes through consistent, mindful effort, not extremes. Align your schedule with wellbeing to sustain future progress.

Affirmation & Gratitude

I give thanks for balance in my routines, creating habits that nurture clarity, health, and sustainable growth today.

Scorpio
19 July 2026

Scorpio, partnerships return to focus. The Sun emphasizes honesty and trust in relationships. Conversations may test patience, but breakthroughs come when you lead with empathy. Passion is present, yet Saturn reminds you: responsibility matters as much as desire. If single, attraction may feel powerful, but time will reveal alignment. Today strengthens bonds built on authenticity.

Affirmation & Gratitude

I am grateful for love and connection, embracing honesty, respect, and patience to nurture deeper, authentic relationships today.

Scorpio
20 July 2026

Scorpio, career matters take center stage. Recognition or added responsibilities may surface, highlighting your resilience and determination. Authority figures notice your persistence—doors could open unexpectedly. Step into visibility with confidence, but ground yourself in authenticity. Avoid comparing your progress to others; your journey is uniquely powerful. Today is about aligning ambition with purpose, ensuring success that's both meaningful and lasting.

Affirmation & Gratitude

I am grateful for career opportunities, embracing authenticity, courage, and integrity to build purposeful and lasting success today.

Scorpio
21 July 2026

Scorpio, the Moon pulls you inward, encouraging rest and reflection. Emotions may feel tender, but they're guiding you toward clarity. Dreams, symbols, or intuitive nudges provide insights. Avoid forcing action; today is for quiet healing and release. Spiritual practices or journaling help you reset. Transformation begins in stillness, and today offers the pause you've needed. Trust the whispers of your soul.

Affirmation & Gratitude

I honor gratitude for stillness and reflection, trusting intuition to bring peace, clarity, and renewal today.

Scorpio
22 July 2026

Scorpio, friendships and community are emphasized. Group conversations or collaborations may inspire fresh opportunities. A friend's encouragement could shift your outlook, opening new paths. Choose uplifting company; avoid draining dynamics. The cosmos reminds you that growth multiplies when shared. Today is about investing in community and embracing collaboration to fuel your journey.

Affirmation & Gratitude

I am grateful for supportive friendships and shared vision, embracing collaboration that inspires creativity, growth, and opportunity today.

Scorpio
23 July 2026

Scorpio, creativity and joy thrive under today's cosmic energy. Venus enhances your magnetism, inspiring romance, passion projects, and playful connections. Passion runs high, but laughter makes love meaningful. Creative expression flows easily, offering breakthroughs if you embrace inspiration. Today, joy is your medicine. Celebrate life unapologetically—love and fun restore your strength and attract blessings.

Affirmation & Gratitude

I embrace gratitude for joy, love, and creativity, allowing passion and playfulness to uplift and inspire my heart today.

Scorpio
24 July 2026

Scorpio, wellness and routines require attention. The Moon emphasizes structure and balance. Work feels busy, but sustainable habits keep you steady. Focus on nourishment, rest, and organization. Avoid perfectionism; transformation grows through small, consistent steps. Today is about creating order in your daily life, ensuring long-term stability and resilience.

Affirmation & Gratitude

I give thanks for balance in my routines, creating habits that nurture health, clarity, and sustainable growth today.

Scorpio
25 July 2026

Scorpio, relationships come into focus. The Sun highlights your partnership zone, urging patience and honesty. Conversations may reveal truths that reshape dynamics. Passion feels magnetic, but Saturn reminds you that maturity and respect sustain intimacy. If single, attraction may spark, but alignment takes time. Today's lesson: love deepens when authenticity leads.

Affirmation & Gratitude

I am grateful for meaningful connections, choosing honesty, respect, and patience to nurture love and trust today.

Scorpio
26 July 2026

Scorpio, career momentum strengthens again. Recognition or advancement opportunities may present themselves. Authority figures or mentors notice your dedication. Step forward boldly but stay humble. Align ambition with purpose—success is stronger when authentic. Your determination speaks louder than words today. Lead with integrity, and your influence will grow naturally.

Affirmation & Gratitude

I am grateful for career growth, embracing authenticity, courage, and humility to create meaningful, lasting success today.

Scorpio
27 July 2026

Scorpio, introspection is emphasized today. The Moon urges rest, reflection, and emotional release. You may feel more sensitive, but clarity emerges when you slow down. Journaling, meditation, or solitude reveals truths you've overlooked. This isn't a day for pushing outward—it's about aligning with your inner compass. Transformation begins in stillness; trust your intuition to guide you toward renewal.

Affirmation & Gratitude

I honor gratitude for rest and reflection, trusting stillness and intuition to bring clarity, peace, and renewal today.

Scorpio
28 July 2026

Scorpio, friendships and community connections energize your spirit. Group projects, networking, or casual conversations could spark new opportunities. Choose uplifting company—your time is precious. A friend's advice may shift your perspective in a meaningful way. The stars remind you: growth multiplies when shared. Today is about embracing collaboration and aligning with supportive people who believe in your vision.

Affirmation & Gratitude

I am grateful for supportive friendships and shared vision, embracing collaboration that inspires creativity, opportunity, and growth today.

Scorpio
29 July 2026

Scorpio, creativity and joy flow strongly. Venus enhances your magnetism, making this a wonderful day for romance, artistic pursuits, or playful fun. Passion feels strong, but laughter deepens connection. Hobbies or self-expression may bring inspiration. The cosmos reminds you that joy is transformative—it restores your balance and draws blessings. Today is about celebrating beauty, love, and creativity without hesitation.

Affirmation & Gratitude

I embrace gratitude for joy, passion, and creativity, allowing love and playfulness to uplift and inspire my spirit today.

Scorpio
30 July 2026

Scorpio, wellness and routines need attention. The Moon emphasizes structure, urging you to refine daily habits for balance. Work feels demanding, but efficiency improves when balanced with self-care. Small adjustments today lead to long-term transformation. Avoid perfectionism—focus on progress, not extremes. By grounding yourself in mindful choices, you create stability and clarity that fuel your future goals.

Affirmation & Gratitude

I give thanks for balance in my routines, creating habits that nurture health, clarity, and sustainable success today.

Scorpio
31 July 2026

Scorpio, relationships move into focus again. The Sun highlights your partnership zone, bringing opportunities for honesty and harmony. Conversations may test patience, but breakthroughs arise when you lead with openness. Passion runs deep, but Saturn insists respect and maturity guide your bonds. Single Scorpios may encounter attraction, but alignment reveals itself with time. Today is about deepening connections through authenticity.

Affirmation & Gratitude

I am grateful for meaningful connections, choosing honesty, patience, and respect to nurture authentic relationships today.

August
2026

Scorpio
01 August 2026

Scorpio, career opportunities may arise today. Recognition or responsibility could put you in the spotlight. Authority figures may notice your persistence and determination. Step forward with confidence, but remain humble. Align ambition with authenticity for long-term success. The cosmos reminds you: your influence is strongest when grounded in purpose. Lead with integrity, and doors open naturally.

Affirmation & Gratitude

I am grateful for career opportunities, embracing authenticity, courage, and humility to create meaningful success today.

Scorpio
02 August 2026

Scorpio, introspection brings clarity. The Moon highlights your inner world, urging reflection and renewal. Emotions may surface, but they're guiding you toward healing. Avoid rushing forward; today is best for quiet practices like journaling, meditation, or time in nature. Growth begins within, and today offers the space to release and reset. Trust your inner wisdom—it knows the next step.

Affirmation & Gratitude

I honor gratitude for stillness and reflection, trusting my intuition to guide peace, healing, and renewal today.

Scorpio
03 August 2026

Scorpio, friendships and community highlight your day. Group conversations or collaborations may bring inspiration for future goals. A friend's perspective could shift how you view a challenge. Choose uplifting company and avoid draining dynamics. Today reminds you that shared vision expands your path. Invest energy where mutual respect thrives, and you'll see new opportunities unfold. Community is a catalyst for your growth now.

Affirmation & Gratitude

I am grateful for supportive friendships and collaborations, embracing shared vision that inspires creativity, opportunity, and growth today.

Scorpio
04 August 2026

Scorpio, creativity and romance thrive under today's stars. Venus amplifies your magnetism, making this an excellent day for love, passion projects, or artistic pursuits. Fun is transformative—it restores balance and energizes your spirit. Relationships deepen when laughter joins intensity. Lean into hobbies or playful activities that make you feel alive. Today is about celebrating love, joy, and creativity without hesitation.

Affirmation & Gratitude

I embrace gratitude for love, joy, and creativity, allowing passion and playfulness to uplift and inspire my spirit today.

Scorpio
05 August 2026

Scorpio, wellness and structure demand attention. The Moon emphasizes discipline, asking you to refine habits for balance. Work feels busy, but sustainable progress matters most. Avoid perfectionism—focus on consistent effort, not extremes. Small adjustments today—better rest, organization, or nourishment—yield powerful long-term results. Today is about grounding yourself in practical choices that support both health and productivity.

Affirmation & Gratitude

I give thanks for balance in my routines, creating habits that nurture clarity, energy, and long-term stability today.

Scorpio
06 August 2026

Scorpio, relationships are in the spotlight. The Sun highlights your partnership zone, urging balance, honesty, and patience. Conversations may reveal truths that reset dynamics. Passion feels magnetic, but Saturn insists on maturity alongside desire. Single Scorpios may feel powerful attraction, but alignment reveals itself over time. Authentic bonds thrive when built on respect and openness.

Affirmation & Gratitude

I am grateful for meaningful connections, choosing honesty, patience, and respect to nurture deeper, authentic relationships today.

Scorpio
07 August 2026

Scorpio, career momentum builds today. Recognition may arrive, or new responsibilities could expand your influence. Authority figures or mentors notice your persistence. Step confidently into visibility but remain humble. Success aligned with authenticity endures. Today asks you to show leadership with integrity, resilience, and purpose. Avoid comparison—your path is unique and powerful.

Affirmation & Gratitude

I am grateful for career opportunities, embracing authenticity, courage, and integrity to create lasting and meaningful success today.

Scorpio
08 August 2026

Scorpio, introspection is highlighted. The Moon pulls you inward, inviting reflection and healing. Emotional sensitivity is heightened—listen closely to what surfaces. Dreams and intuitive nudges carry guidance. Today isn't for outward push but for inner renewal. By making space for silence, you align with transformation. Trust that your intuition already holds the answers you seek.

Affirmation & Gratitude

I honor gratitude for stillness and reflection, trusting intuition to bring peace, clarity, and renewal today.

Scorpio
09 August 2026

Scorpio, friendships and community connections energize you. Networking, group projects, or casual conversations could spark opportunity. A friend's support may open a new path forward. Choose circles that uplift you—shared vision multiplies growth. Today is about leaning into collaboration and celebrating the power of community. Surround yourself with people who value your depth.

Affirmation & Gratitude

I am grateful for supportive friendships and shared vision, embracing collaboration that inspires creativity, growth, and opportunity today.

Scorpio
10 August 2026

Scorpio, creativity and romance light up your day. Venus enhances your magnetism, inspiring love, playfulness, and artistic expression. Passion flows strongly, but joy makes it meaningful. Relationships thrive when shared with laughter as much as depth. Creative pursuits flourish—follow inspiration. The stars remind you that fun is transformative, restoring balance and attracting blessings. Today is about celebrating beauty, love, and joy without hesitation.

Affirmation & Gratitude

I embrace gratitude for love, joy, and creativity, allowing passion and playfulness to uplift and inspire my spirit today.

Scorpio
11 August 2026

Scorpio, health and structure require your attention. The Moon emphasizes routines, urging you to refine habits for long-term stability. Work feels demanding, but balance is key—don't sacrifice rest or nourishment. Transformation grows through small, consistent steps, not extremes. Today, focus on practical actions that ground your energy and strengthen your clarity. Discipline today becomes resilience tomorrow.

Affirmation & Gratitude

I give thanks for balance in my routines, creating habits that nurture clarity, vitality, and long-term success today.

Scorpio
12 August 2026

Scorpio, relationships dominate the cosmic focus. The Sun emphasizes your partnership zone, encouraging honesty and balance. Conversations may feel revealing, but they deepen understanding when handled with empathy. Passion is strong, yet Saturn reminds you that maturity builds stability. Single Scorpios may feel drawn toward magnetic attraction, but clarity takes time. Authentic love grows through openness and respect.

Affirmation & Gratitude

I am grateful for meaningful connections, choosing honesty, patience, and empathy to nurture deeper, authentic relationships today.

Scorpio
13 August 2026

Scorpio, career matters are emphasized today. Recognition or opportunity may arise, validating your persistence. Authority figures may notice your resilience. Step forward confidently, but ground yourself in authenticity. Avoid comparing your progress to others; your path is unique. Today is about aligning ambition with purpose. Success is most enduring when built on integrity, resilience, and truth.

Affirmation & Gratitude

I am grateful for career opportunities, embracing authenticity, courage, and integrity to create lasting and meaningful success today.

Scorpio
14 August 2026

Scorpio, introspection is highlighted. The Moon draws you inward, urging rest, reflection, and release. Emotional sensitivity may heighten, but it's guiding you toward clarity. Avoid forcing outcomes; today is for inner healing. Journaling, meditation, or solitude helps you recalibrate. Growth often begins in stillness. Trust your intuition—it carries the answers you need.

Affirmation & Gratitude

I honor gratitude for stillness and reflection, trusting intuition to bring clarity, peace, and renewal today.

Scorpio
15 August 2026

Scorpio, friendships and community energize your path. Collaborations, conversations, or gatherings may spark inspiration. A friend's encouragement could shift your outlook and open opportunities. Choose uplifting company —your energy is too precious for negativity. Today's cosmic reminder: community amplifies growth. Invest in connections that align with your spirit.

Affirmation & Gratitude

I am grateful for supportive friendships and shared vision, embracing collaboration that inspires creativity, opportunity, and growth today.

Scorpio
16 August 2026

Scorpio, creativity and joy flourish under today's cosmic influence. Venus highlights your playful side, making this a perfect day for romance, art, or laughter. Passion runs high, but authenticity ensures depth. Allow yourself to celebrate beauty, love, and fun unapologetically. Joy is not a luxury—it's a necessity. Today, lean into what makes your heart feel alive.

Affirmation & Gratitude

I embrace gratitude for joy, love, and creativity, allowing passion and play to uplift and renew my spirit today.

Scorpio
17 August 2026

Scorpio, wellness and routines take priority. The Moon emphasizes discipline, asking you to refine habits that support your health and productivity. Work requires focus, but balance prevents burnout. Sustainable progress grows through consistent effort, not extremes. Today, ground yourself with practical actions like organization, nourishment, or rest. Small improvements create big shifts over time.

Affirmation & Gratitude

I give thanks for balance in my routines, creating habits that nurture clarity, vitality, and sustainable success today.

Scorpio
18 August 2026

Scorpio, partnerships take center stage. The Sun emphasizes your relationship sector, urging honesty, patience, and respect. Conversations may reveal truths that deepen understanding. Passion feels strong, but Saturn reminds you that stability requires maturity. For singles, attraction may feel magnetic, yet clarity takes time. Authentic intimacy thrives when built on openness and trust.

Affirmation & Gratitude

I am grateful for meaningful connections, choosing honesty, patience, and respect to nurture authentic love and trust today.

Scorpio
19 August 2026

Scorpio, career momentum builds. Recognition or responsibility may place you in the spotlight. Authority figures may notice your persistence and determination. Step forward confidently, but remain grounded in authenticity. Avoid comparison—your path is unique. Today, align ambition with purpose, ensuring long-term success. Leadership shines brightest when rooted in truth.

Affirmation & Gratitude

I am grateful for career opportunities, embracing authenticity, courage, and integrity to create lasting and meaningful success today.

Scorpio
20 August 2026

Scorpio, introspection calls. The Moon encourages rest, reflection, and emotional release. You may feel sensitive, but clarity comes through stillness. Avoid forcing outcomes; trust your intuition. Journaling or meditation may provide insight into a current challenge. Transformation begins within, and today offers space to reset your spirit. Embrace healing through quiet reflection.

Affirmation & Gratitude

I honor gratitude for stillness and reflection, trusting my inner wisdom to guide clarity, renewal, and peace today.

Scorpio
21 August 2026

Scorpio, friendships and community bring energy. Conversations or collaborations may spark inspiration for the future. A friend's perspective could offer valuable support. Choose uplifting company, and invest only where there is mutual respect. Today reminds you: community amplifies growth and strengthens your vision. Shared goals bring greater momentum than solitary effort.

Affirmation & Gratitude

I am grateful for supportive friendships and shared vision, embracing collaboration that inspires growth, creativity, and opportunity today.

Scorpio
22 August 2026

Scorpio, creativity and romance shine brightly. Venus enhances your magnetism, making this a perfect day for love, laughter, and artistic pursuits. Passion is strong, but joy gives it depth. Creative projects flow easily, and inspiration surrounds you. Don't dismiss fun as frivolous—it restores balance and uplifts your spirit. Celebrate beauty and connection unapologetically.

Affirmation & Gratitude

I embrace gratitude for love, joy, and creativity, allowing passion and playfulness to uplift and inspire my spirit today.

Scorpio
23 August 2026

Scorpio, wellness and order are highlighted again. The cosmos urges you to refine daily habits and focus on structure. Small improvements—better rest, nourishment, or organization—create lasting transformation. Work requires discipline, but avoid overexertion. Balance ensures both productivity and wellbeing. Today is about creating stability through mindful choices that fuel your growth long term.

Affirmation & Gratitude

I give thanks for balance in daily life, creating habits that nurture clarity, health, and long-term resilience today.

Scorpio
24 August 2026

Scorpio, relationships come to the forefront. The Sun and Moon emphasize partnerships, asking for patience, honesty, and balance. Conversations may reveal truths that reshape dynamics. Passion feels strong, but Saturn reminds you that maturity and responsibility sustain intimacy. For singles, attraction feels magnetic, but discernment matters most. Authenticity in love and friendship is your guiding star today.

Affirmation & Gratitude

I am grateful for meaningful relationships, choosing honesty, respect, and patience to nurture authentic love and deeper bonds today.

Scorpio
25 August 2026

Scorpio, career matters are highlighted. Recognition or advancement may come your way. Authority figures or mentors could offer guidance. Step confidently into visibility but stay humble. Align ambition with integrity, not comparison. Your path is unique, and today you're reminded that true success is built on authenticity, resilience, and purpose. Own your power gracefully.

Affirmation & Gratitude

I give thanks for opportunities in my career, embracing authenticity, courage, and integrity to create meaningful and lasting success today.

Scorpio
26 August 2026

Scorpio, introspection is emphasized today. The Moon urges you to slow down, reflect, and release emotional clutter. Pay attention to dreams or symbols—they hold guidance. Avoid rushing outwardly; this is a day for healing and inner clarity. Spiritual practices, journaling, or meditation will restore peace. Transformation often begins quietly, in moments of stillness and surrender.

Affirmation & Gratitude

I honor gratitude for stillness and reflection, trusting my inner wisdom to guide clarity, renewal, and peace today.

Scorpio
27 August 2026

Scorpio, friendships and social connections spark inspiration. A group activity, conversation, or collaboration may open new opportunities. Choose circles that uplift you—avoid draining dynamics. A friend's encouragement could shift your perspective and help you see potential you overlooked. Today reminds you that growth expands when shared with supportive allies.

Affirmation & Gratitude

I am grateful for supportive friendships and shared vision, embracing collaboration that inspires creativity, opportunity, and growth today.

Scorpio
28 August 2026

Scorpio, creativity and romance flourish today. Venus amplifies your charm, inspiring passion projects, love, and playful energy. Relationships thrive when paired with laughter and authenticity. Creative expression flows easily, offering breakthroughs if you lean into inspiration. The cosmos reminds you that joy is a transformative force—it restores balance and fuels your spirit. Celebrate love and beauty.

Affirmation & Gratitude

I embrace gratitude for love, joy, and creativity, allowing passion and playfulness to uplift and inspire my spirit today.

Scorpio
29 August 2026

Scorpio, wellness and daily order are emphasized. The stars urge you to refine habits and create balance. Work requires focus, but self-care sustains long-term success. Small adjustments today—organization, rest, or nourishment—set you on the path toward transformation. Avoid perfectionism; progress is enough. Today is about grounding yourself in practices that strengthen resilience.

Affirmation & Gratitude

I give thanks for balance in my routines, creating habits that nurture clarity, health, and sustainable growth today.

Scorpio
30 August 2026

Scorpio, partnerships return to focus. Conversations may test patience, but they're opportunities for deeper understanding. Passion feels magnetic, but Saturn reminds you that maturity ensures longevity. Authentic intimacy thrives on openness, respect, and balance. Whether in romance, friendship, or work, today asks you to listen deeply and respond truthfully. Love strengthens when vulnerability leads.

Affirmation & Gratitude

I am grateful for love and connection, embracing honesty, patience, and empathy to nurture authentic, lasting relationships today.

Scorpio
31 August 2026

Scorpio, career momentum builds today. Recognition or responsibility may spotlight your persistence. Authority figures notice your resilience, opening doors for advancement. Align ambition with authenticity—success built on truth lasts. Avoid comparing your path to others; your journey is unique. Today is about embodying leadership with humility and purpose. Trust that your efforts are planting seeds for long-term rewards.

Affirmation & Gratitude

I am grateful for career opportunities, embracing courage, authenticity, and integrity to create lasting and meaningful success today.

September 2026

Scorpio
01 September 2026

Scorpio, introspection takes focus. The Moon pulls you inward, encouraging reflection, release, and renewal. Emotions may feel tender, but they carry guidance. Dreams, symbols, or synchronicities offer insight. Today is not for pushing forward—it's for resting and realigning. Journaling, meditation, or solitude helps uncover truths you've overlooked. Transformation begins in silence; trust your intuition to light the way.

Affirmation & Gratitude

I honor gratitude for stillness and reflection, trusting intuition to reveal clarity, peace, and renewal today.

Scorpio
02 September 2026

Scorpio, friendships and community energize you. Conversations, group activities, or collaborations may spark new opportunities. A friend's perspective could inspire you to see things differently. Surround yourself with uplifting company—your time is too valuable for negativity. Today, your path expands when aligned with supportive allies. Shared vision multiplies growth and amplifies your confidence.

Affirmation & Gratitude

I am grateful for supportive friendships and shared vision, embracing collaboration that inspires creativity, growth, and opportunity today.

Scorpio
03 September 2026

Scorpio, creativity and romance thrive. Venus amplifies your magnetism, making today ideal for passion, artistic projects, or playful self-expression. Relationships deepen when paired with laughter and joy. Creative breakthroughs may come easily—trust your inspiration. Fun isn't frivolous; it restores your energy and draws blessings closer. Today is about embracing beauty, love, and creativity unapologetically. Celebrate what makes you feel alive.

Affirmation & Gratitude

I embrace gratitude for joy, love, and creativity, allowing passion and playfulness to uplift and inspire my spirit today.

Scorpio
04 September 2026

Scorpio, wellness and routines take focus. The cosmos encourages balance between work and self-care. Productivity feels high, but sustainability matters more than speed. Avoid perfectionism—consistent progress creates lasting transformation. Today is about grounding yourself in healthy habits and refining structure. By honoring your wellbeing alongside responsibilities, you prepare yourself for long-term stability and success.

Affirmation & Gratitude

I give thanks for balance in my routines, creating habits that nurture health, clarity, and sustainable progress today.

Scorpio
05 September 2026

Scorpio, relationships move into focus again. Conversations may reveal truths that deepen trust or reset boundaries. Passion feels magnetic, but Saturn reminds you that maturity matters most. Single Scorpios may encounter attraction, but time reveals alignment. In all connections, intimacy thrives when respect and openness lead. Today is about strengthening relationships by leading with authenticity and patience.

Affirmation & Gratitude

I am grateful for love and connection, embracing honesty, patience, and empathy to nurture deeper, authentic relationships today.

Scorpio
06 September 2026

Scorpio, career recognition may arrive today. Authority figures or mentors could acknowledge your persistence. New responsibilities may expand your influence. Step forward with confidence—your resilience is shining. Align ambition with integrity, and avoid comparison. Today asks you to show leadership with humility and purpose. Your influence strengthens when grounded in authenticity. Success built this way endures.

Affirmation & Gratitude

I am grateful for opportunities in my career, embracing authenticity, courage, and integrity to build meaningful success today.

Scorpio
07 September 2026

Scorpio, introspection is strong today. The Moon highlights your inner world, urging you to release emotional clutter and restore balance. Sensitivity is heightened, but it's guiding you toward clarity. Avoid external pressure—this is a day for journaling, meditation, or solitude. By honoring stillness, you align with your deepest truth. Healing and renewal come when you embrace silence. Trust the wisdom you uncover.

Affirmation & Gratitude

I honor gratitude for stillness and reflection, trusting my intuition to reveal clarity, renewal, and inner peace today.

Scorpio
08 September 2026

Scorpio, friendships and community light up your day. Conversations or group projects may spark fresh ideas. Surround yourself with uplifting, supportive people. A friend's encouragement could shift your perspective in a meaningful way. Collaboration multiplies your growth and widens your reach. Choose alliances wisely—invest energy where respect is mutual. Today reminds you that shared vision inspires long-term success.

Affirmation & Gratitude

I am grateful for supportive friendships and shared vision, embracing collaboration that inspires creativity, growth, and opportunity today.

Scorpio
09 September 2026

Scorpio, creativity and romance thrive. Venus enhances your magnetism, making this an excellent day for passion, playfulness, and artistic pursuits. Love deepens when laughter balances intensity. Creative breakthroughs may arrive unexpectedly—trust your inspiration. Fun is transformative, not frivolous. Today is about celebrating beauty, connection, and joy unapologetically. Let passion and creativity fuel your spirit and attract new blessings.

Affirmation & Gratitude

I embrace gratitude for joy, love, and creativity, allowing passion and playfulness to uplift and inspire my spirit today.

Scorpio
10 September 2026

Scorpio, wellness and order require attention. The Moon emphasizes routines, encouraging structure and discipline. Small, consistent steps today bring long-term growth. Work feels busy, but don't sacrifice self-care. Balance responsibilities with nourishment and rest. Transformation comes from steady progress, not extremes. Today is about grounding yourself in habits that support clarity, health, and productivity.

Affirmation & Gratitude

I give thanks for balance in my routines, creating habits that nurture health, clarity, and sustainable progress today.

Scorpio
11 September 2026

Scorpio, partnerships are emphasized. The Sun highlights your relationship sector, encouraging balance, patience, and honesty. Conversations may feel revealing, but they strengthen bonds. Passion runs deep, but Saturn reminds you that maturity sustains intimacy. Single Scorpios may feel drawn to someone magnetic, but alignment takes time. Authentic love flourishes through openness, respect, and trust.

Affirmation & Gratitude

I am grateful for meaningful connections, choosing honesty, patience, and respect to nurture authentic relationships today.

Scorpio
12 September 2026

Scorpio, career energy builds. Recognition, advancement, or new responsibility may surface. Authority figures or mentors could acknowledge your resilience. Step forward confidently, but stay humble. Align ambition with integrity, and avoid comparing your journey with others. Today's cosmic reminder: true success is built on authenticity, persistence, and purpose. Your influence grows when grounded in truth.

Affirmation & Gratitude

I am grateful for career opportunities, embracing authenticity, courage, and integrity to create lasting success today.

Scorpio
13 September 2026

Scorpio, introspection calls again. The Moon encourages solitude, journaling, or meditation to gain clarity. Emotional sensitivity may heighten, but it's guiding you toward release and renewal. Avoid rushing decisions; let your intuition speak. Healing begins when you honor your inner world. By listening inward, you uncover answers that move you forward with strength and balance. Trust the wisdom unfolding.

Affirmation & Gratitude

I honor gratitude for stillness and reflection, trusting my intuition to bring clarity, healing, and renewal today.

Scorpio
14 September 2026

Scorpio, friendships and community energize you. Conversations, collaborations, or networking may spark exciting opportunities. Surround yourself with allies who uplift your vision. A friend's perspective could shift how you view a challenge. Shared goals strengthen your path and bring momentum. The cosmos reminds you: growth expands when it's nurtured in community. Choose wisely where you invest your energy today.

Affirmation & Gratitude

I am grateful for supportive friendships and shared vision, embracing collaboration that inspires creativity, growth, and opportunity today.

Scorpio
15 September 2026

Scorpio, creativity and romance flourish under today's stars. Venus amplifies your magnetism, making this a wonderful day for love, laughter, and artistic pursuits. Passion flows, but it's joy that deepens connection. Creative projects may bring breakthroughs if you trust your inspiration. Celebrate love and playfulness unapologetically—joy is transformative, not frivolous. Today invites you to shine with authenticity.

Affirmation & Gratitude

I embrace gratitude for love, joy, and creativity, allowing passion and playfulness to uplift and inspire my spirit today.

Scorpio
16 September 2026

Scorpio, wellness and structure require focus. The Moon highlights routines, urging you to refine daily habits for better balance. Work feels busy, but sustainability matters more than speed. Avoid perfectionism; small, consistent changes lead to lasting transformation. Today is about grounding yourself in practices that nurture body, mind, and spirit. Balance creates strength for long-term growth.

Affirmation & Gratitude

I give thanks for balance in my routines, creating habits that nurture clarity, health, and stability today.

Scorpio
17 September 2026

Scorpio, relationships are emphasized today. The Sun highlights your partnership zone, bringing opportunities for honest conversations and deeper trust. Passion feels magnetic, but Saturn insists on maturity alongside desire. For singles, attraction may feel strong, but alignment unfolds with time. True intimacy thrives when openness and respect lead the way. This is a day for strengthening love through patience.

Affirmation & Gratitude

I am grateful for meaningful relationships, choosing honesty, respect, and patience to nurture authentic, lasting bonds today.

Scorpio
18 September 2026

Scorpio, career matters move into focus. Recognition or new opportunities may highlight your persistence. Authority figures may notice your determination. Step forward confidently, but lead with humility. Avoid comparing yourself with others; your journey is uniquely powerful. Success rooted in authenticity and purpose lasts. Today reminds you that leadership shines brightest when grounded in truth and integrity.

Affirmation & Gratitude

I am grateful for career opportunities, embracing authenticity, courage, and integrity to create meaningful and lasting success today.

Scorpio
19 September 2026

Scorpio, the Moon emphasizes introspection again. You may feel called to withdraw and recharge emotionally. Dreams, symbols, or intuition offer guidance now. Avoid overextending yourself; instead, focus on rest and renewal. Spiritual practices or quiet time help you release emotional clutter. By pausing, you make space for clarity and growth. Trust the silence—it carries answers you need.

Affirmation & Gratitude

I honor gratitude for stillness and reflection, trusting my inner wisdom to guide clarity, peace, and renewal today.

Scorpio
20 September 2026

Scorpio, friendships and alliances are emphasized today. Conversations or group efforts may reveal opportunities for shared success. Surround yourself with allies who respect your depth and vision. Collaboration can bring momentum, but choose wisely where you invest energy. A friend's encouragement may spark new ideas. Today reminds you that community multiplies growth and strengthens your path.

Affirmation & Gratitude

I am grateful for supportive friendships and shared vision, embracing collaboration that inspires creativity, opportunity, and growth today.

Scorpio
21 September 2026

Scorpio, creativity and romance shine under today's stars. Venus enhances your magnetism, making this a perfect day for passion, joy, and expression. Love deepens when mixed with laughter. Creative pursuits may bring breakthroughs—trust your instincts. The cosmos reminds you that joy is not trivial—it is transformative. Today is about embracing beauty, love, and playfulness unapologetically. Celebrate what inspires your soul.

Affirmation & Gratitude

I embrace gratitude for love, joy, and creativity, allowing passion and playfulness to uplift and inspire my spirit today.

Scorpio
22 September 2026

Scorpio, routines and wellness require attention. The Moon emphasizes structure and discipline, asking you to refine habits for balance. Work feels demanding, but consistency beats extremes. Small changes—better nourishment, rest, or organization—yield long-term rewards. Today is about creating stability through mindful choices. By aligning effort with wellbeing, you prepare yourself for sustainable growth and clarity.

Affirmation & Gratitude

I give thanks for balance in my routines, creating habits that nurture health, clarity, and long-term success today.

Scorpio
23 September 2026

Scorpio, relationships are highlighted. The Sun emphasizes balance, honesty, and maturity in partnerships. Conversations may bring clarity, offering opportunities to reset or deepen bonds. Passion feels strong, but Saturn reminds you that lasting intimacy is built on responsibility and respect. For singles, attraction may spark, but patience reveals true alignment. Today is about strengthening love through authenticity.

Affirmation & Gratitude

I am grateful for meaningful relationships, choosing honesty, patience, and respect to nurture authentic and lasting connections today.

Scorpio
24 September 2026

Scorpio, career matters gain momentum. Recognition, advancement, or responsibility may arise. Authority figures may acknowledge your persistence and determination. Step confidently into visibility, but ground yourself in integrity. Avoid comparison—your journey is uniquely powerful. Today, leadership and authenticity set you apart. Success rooted in truth lasts, and your influence grows when you embody your calling.

Affirmation & Gratitude

I am grateful for career opportunities, embracing authenticity, courage, and integrity to create meaningful and lasting success today.

Scorpio
25 September 2026

Scorpio, introspection is emphasized. The Moon urges quiet reflection, inviting you to release old emotions and restore balance. Pay attention to dreams and subtle signs—they hold important messages. Avoid rushing into action. Today is for journaling, meditation, or spiritual renewal. By honoring your inner world, you prepare for transformation. Trust the silence; it carries the answers you've been seeking.

Affirmation & Gratitude

I honor gratitude for stillness and reflection, trusting intuition to reveal clarity, healing, and renewal today.

Scorpio
26 September 2026

Scorpio, friendships and community connections energize your path. Networking, group conversations, or collaborations may open new opportunities. Choose alliances carefully—your energy is valuable. A friend's support could shift your perspective positively. The cosmos reminds you that teamwork expands your reach and strengthens your vision. Today is about investing in connections that align with your values.

Affirmation & Gratitude

I am grateful for supportive friendships and shared vision, embracing collaboration that inspires creativity, opportunity, and growth today.

Scorpio
27 September 2026

Scorpio, creativity and joy take center stage. Venus heightens your magnetism, drawing love, laughter, and artistic expression into your orbit. Relationships thrive when paired with playfulness and lightness. Creative pursuits flourish—trust your inspiration. Fun isn't a distraction; it restores balance and reminds you of life's beauty. Today, passion flows effortlessly, and joy becomes transformative.

Affirmation & Gratitude

I embrace gratitude for love, joy, and creativity, allowing passion and playfulness to uplift and renew my spirit today.

Scorpio
28 September 2026

Scorpio, wellness and discipline require your focus. The Moon emphasizes balance in your daily routines. Small, intentional changes today lead to long-term transformation. Work demands attention, but don't neglect self-care. Sustainable growth comes from steady progress, not extremes. Align body, mind, and spirit with healthy choices. Today, grounding yourself in simple habits ensures clarity and resilience for the future.

Affirmation & Gratitude

I give thanks for balance in my routines, creating habits that nurture health, clarity, and long-term strength today.

Scorpio
29 September 2026

Scorpio, relationships come into focus. The Sun emphasizes honesty, patience, and balance in your connections. Conversations may uncover truths that reshape dynamics. Passion feels magnetic, but Saturn insists maturity and respect sustain intimacy. Single Scorpios may feel powerful attraction, but discernment reveals alignment over time. Today is about deepening bonds through openness and authenticity.

Affirmation & Gratitude

I am grateful for meaningful connections, choosing honesty, patience, and respect to nurture authentic, lasting relationships today.

Scorpio
30 September 2026

Scorpio, career matters are emphasized today. Recognition or new responsibilities may highlight your persistence and determination. Authority figures or mentors notice your resilience. Step into visibility confidently, but stay humble. Align ambition with authenticity for long-term success. Avoid comparison—your journey is uniquely powerful. Today asks you to lead with purpose, integrity, and courage.

Affirmation & Gratitude

I am grateful for career opportunities, embracing authenticity, courage, and integrity to create lasting and meaningful success today.

October 2026

Scorpio
01 October 2026

Scorpio, introspection is powerful now. The Moon highlights your inner world, urging quiet reflection, release, and healing. Emotional sensitivity may rise, but it carries wisdom. Pay attention to dreams or intuitive whispers—they hold answers. Avoid rushing outwardly; today is for spiritual practices or solitude. Transformation begins in silence. Trust the process of renewal.

Affirmation & Gratitude

I honor gratitude for stillness and reflection, trusting my intuition to bring clarity, peace, and renewal today.

Scorpio
02 October 2026

Scorpio, friendships and alliances are energized. Social interactions, collaborations, or group projects may spark opportunity. A friend's encouragement could shift your outlook positively. Choose uplifting company—avoid draining circles. Today is about amplifying growth through teamwork and shared vision. The cosmos reminds you that community strengthens your journey. Invest your energy where respect and inspiration thrive.

Affirmation & Gratitude

I am grateful for supportive friendships and shared vision, embracing collaboration that inspires creativity, growth, and opportunity today.

Scorpio
03 October 2026

Scorpio, creativity and romance flourish again. Venus makes you magnetic, inspiring love, joy, and artistic expression. Passion flows easily, but laughter and playfulness give it depth. Creative breakthroughs may come if you embrace inspiration. The cosmos encourages you to celebrate beauty and connection fully. Today's energy reminds you: joy is transformative—embrace it unapologetically.

Affirmation & Gratitude

I embrace gratitude for love, joy, and creativity, allowing passion and playfulness to uplift and inspire my spirit today.

Scorpio
04 October 2026

Scorpio, wellness and routines take the spotlight. The Moon emphasizes structure, asking you to refine habits that sustain energy and focus. Work feels demanding, but small, steady improvements bring long-term strength. Avoid extremes—balance is your ally. Nourishment, rest, and order support clarity today. By grounding yourself in mindful choices, you create stability to handle greater responsibilities ahead.

Affirmation & Gratitude

I give thanks for balance in my routines, creating habits that nurture health, clarity, and resilience today.

Scorpio
05 October 2026

Scorpio, relationships deepen under today's skies. The Sun highlights partnerships, asking for patience, empathy, and openness. Conversations may bring truths that reshape dynamics, strengthening bonds if handled with honesty. Passion flows strongly, but Saturn insists maturity and respect sustain intimacy. Single Scorpios may feel magnetic attraction, but alignment reveals itself in time. Authentic love thrives in truth.

Affirmation & Gratitude

I am grateful for meaningful connections, choosing honesty, patience, and respect to nurture authentic, lasting relationships today.

Scorpio
06 October 2026

Scorpio, career momentum builds. Recognition, advancement, or new responsibility could arise, highlighting your persistence. Authority figures or mentors may acknowledge your determination. Step forward confidently, but ground ambition in integrity. Avoid comparisons; your path is unique. Today is about showing leadership authentically and aligning success with your deeper calling. Success built on truth endures.

Affirmation & Gratitude

I am grateful for career opportunities, embracing authenticity, courage, and integrity to create meaningful and lasting success today.

Scorpio
07 October 2026

Scorpio, introspection and renewal dominate today. The Moon pulls you inward, urging rest and quiet reflection. Emotions may feel heightened, but they guide you toward healing. Journaling, meditation, or solitude helps uncover clarity. Avoid rushing; this is a day for spiritual practices and inner alignment. Transformation often begins in silence—trust the wisdom unfolding from within.

Affirmation & Gratitude

I honor gratitude for stillness and reflection, trusting my intuition to bring peace, clarity, and renewal today.

Scorpio
08 October 2026

Scorpio, friendships and social circles bring inspiration. Conversations or collaborations may spark ideas that expand your vision. A friend's encouragement could offer new possibilities. Surround yourself with uplifting company—avoid draining dynamics. The cosmos reminds you that shared vision amplifies success. Today is about aligning with community and investing your energy where mutual respect thrives.

Affirmation & Gratitude

I am grateful for supportive friendships and shared vision, embracing collaboration that inspires creativity, growth, and opportunity today.

Scorpio
09 October 2026

Scorpio, creativity and romance flourish. Venus amplifies your magnetism, inspiring love, joy, and artistic expression. Passion is strong, but playfulness gives it meaning. Creative breakthroughs may come easily if you trust your inspiration. Celebrate beauty and connection unapologetically—joy is transformative, not frivolous. Today, laughter and love restore balance, reminding you that joy is as powerful as intensity.

Affirmation & Gratitude

I embrace gratitude for love, joy, and creativity, allowing passion and playfulness to uplift and inspire my spirit today.

Scorpio
10 October 2026

Scorpio, wellness and daily order take focus again. The Moon emphasizes discipline and consistency. Work may feel demanding, but balance is key. Sustainable progress grows through small, practical steps. Avoid overexertion—rest is just as vital as productivity. Today, grounding yourself in healthy routines ensures clarity and stability. Transformation builds on consistency, not extremes.

Affirmation & Gratitude

I give thanks for balance in my daily life, creating habits that nurture health, clarity, and strength today.

Scorpio
11 October 2026

Scorpio, relationships are emphasized today. The Sun highlights partnerships, encouraging honesty, patience, and balance. Conversations may reveal truths that shift dynamics, strengthening bonds through openness. Passion runs high, but Saturn insists that maturity sustains intimacy. If single, attraction may feel magnetic, but discernment ensures long-term alignment. Today's lesson: authenticity is the cornerstone of meaningful love.

Affirmation & Gratitude

I am grateful for meaningful relationships, choosing honesty, patience, and respect to nurture authentic and lasting love today.

Scorpio
12 October 2026

Scorpio, career momentum builds again. Recognition or responsibility may arise, spotlighting your determination. Authority figures may notice your persistence and open new doors. Step forward confidently, but lead with integrity. Avoid comparing your path to others—your journey is uniquely powerful. Today is about aligning ambition with your purpose. Success grounded in authenticity endures.

Affirmation & Gratitude

I am grateful for career opportunities, embracing authenticity, courage, and integrity to create meaningful and lasting success today.

Scorpio
13 October 2026

Scorpio, introspection is highlighted. The Moon invites you to slow down, reflect, and release emotional clutter. Sensitivity may feel high, but it's a compass for clarity. Today is ideal for meditation, journaling, or solitude. By creating quiet space, you allow renewal. Transformation begins within, and this is your chance to reset your inner landscape. Trust yourself.

Affirmation & Gratitude

I honor gratitude for stillness and reflection, trusting my inner wisdom to bring peace, clarity, and renewal today.

Scorpio
14 October 2026

Scorpio, friendships and alliances bring energy. Collaborations or group conversations may spark fresh opportunities. A friend's perspective could help you see new possibilities. Invest in connections that uplift and support you. Today's cosmic message: community strengthens your journey and amplifies your vision. Shared effort brings momentum where solitary striving cannot. Surround yourself with supportive allies.

Affirmation & Gratitude

I am grateful for supportive friendships and shared vision, embracing collaboration that inspires creativity, growth, and opportunity today.

Scorpio
15 October 2026

Scorpio, creativity and romance thrive. Venus enhances your magnetism, inspiring love, joy, and artistic expression. Passion flows strongly, but laughter and playfulness add depth. Creative breakthroughs may arrive if you embrace inspiration without hesitation. Today is about celebrating beauty unapologetically and allowing joy to renew your spirit. Fun restores balance and draws new blessings closer.

Affirmation & Gratitude

I embrace gratitude for love, joy, and creativity, allowing passion and playfulness to uplift and inspire my spirit today.

Scorpio
16 October 2026

Scorpio, routines and wellness require attention. The Moon emphasizes structure, encouraging you to refine daily habits. Small, consistent adjustments lead to long-term stability. Work may feel busy, but balance ensures clarity. Avoid perfectionism—progress is enough. Today is about creating mindful rhythms that support body, mind, and spirit equally. Steady choices now build future resilience.

Affirmation & Gratitude

I give thanks for balance in my routines, creating habits that nurture health, clarity, and sustainable growth today.

Scorpio
17 October 2026

Scorpio, relationships come into focus once more. The Sun highlights partnerships, urging patience, empathy, and openness. Conversations may strengthen trust or reset boundaries. Passion is magnetic, but Saturn insists responsibility and respect deepen intimacy. For singles, attraction may spark, but time reveals alignment. Authenticity is your guide—true love flourishes in honesty and trust.

Affirmation & Gratitude

I am grateful for love and connection, embracing honesty, patience, and respect to nurture authentic relationships today.

Scorpio
18 October 2026

Scorpio, career focus intensifies. Recognition or responsibility may arrive, placing you in the spotlight. Authority figures notice your persistence, opening new opportunities. Step into leadership with humility and integrity. Success today is about more than status—it's about aligning ambition with purpose. Avoid comparison; your journey is unique and powerful. By embodying authenticity, you inspire respect and trust.

Affirmation & Gratitude

I am grateful for career opportunities, embracing authenticity, courage, and integrity to create meaningful and lasting success today.

Scorpio
19 October 2026

Scorpio, introspection is highlighted. The Moon encourages rest, reflection, and emotional release. You may feel sensitive, but this sensitivity guides you toward truth. Dreams, synchronicities, or subtle feelings offer clarity. Avoid forcing progress—today is about healing and renewal. Journaling or meditation can help uncover insights. Trust your intuition to reveal what needs release.

Affirmation & Gratitude

I honor gratitude for stillness and reflection, trusting intuition to bring clarity, healing, and renewal today.

Scorpio
20 October 2026

Scorpio, friendships and community inspire growth. Group conversations or collaborations may spark creative solutions. A friend's encouragement could provide clarity and motivation. Today reminds you that support systems amplify your journey. Choose uplifting allies and step away from draining dynamics. Shared vision multiplies opportunities and strengthens your sense of belonging. Community is your foundation for expansion.

Affirmation & Gratitude

I am grateful for supportive friendships and shared vision, embracing collaboration that inspires creativity, growth, and opportunity today.

Scorpio
21 October 2026

Scorpio, creativity and romance thrive. Venus amplifies your magnetism, inspiring joy, love, and artistic pursuits. Relationships flourish when paired with lightheartedness and laughter. Creative projects bring breakthroughs if you embrace inspiration without hesitation. The cosmos reminds you that joy is healing—it restores balance and attracts blessings. Today, celebrate love and self-expression fully.

Affirmation & Gratitude

I embrace gratitude for love, joy, and creativity, allowing passion and playfulness to uplift and inspire my spirit today.

Scorpio
22 October 2026

Scorpio, wellness and routines require your focus. The Moon emphasizes balance and discipline in daily life. Small, consistent adjustments bring long-term results. Work may feel demanding, but avoid sacrificing rest or nourishment. Transformation grows through sustainable effort. Today's lesson: progress is more important than perfection. Ground yourself in routines that nurture clarity, health, and stability.

Affirmation & Gratitude

I give thanks for balance in my routines, creating habits that nurture health, clarity, and sustainable growth today.

Scorpio
23 October 2026

Scorpio, relationships are emphasized again as the Sun moves into your sign. This shift awakens your magnetism and intensifies focus on love, balance, and personal truth. Conversations may feel transformative, offering breakthroughs in intimacy or clarity in partnerships. Passion runs deep, but responsibility ensures stability. Today, authentic love thrives when guided by honesty, respect, and patience.

Affirmation & Gratitude

I am grateful for meaningful relationships, choosing honesty, patience, and respect to nurture authentic love and connection today.

Scorpio
24 October 2026

Scorpio, the Sun officially illuminates your sign, marking the start of your solar season. This is your personal new year—a time of renewal, empowerment, and self-expression. Energy surges, making you magnetic and determined. Use today to set intentions for the year ahead. The cosmos aligns with your strength, urging you to step boldly into authenticity.

Affirmation & Gratitude

I give thanks for personal renewal and empowerment, embracing authenticity, courage, and purpose as I step into a powerful new cycle today.

Scorpio
25 October 2026

Scorpio, the Sun in your sign amplifies your presence and power. Confidence surges, making this an ideal day to pursue goals or express truth. Others notice your magnetism—use it wisely. The cosmos urges you to align with authenticity, shedding what no longer serves. Today's energy marks a turning point, fueling renewal and courage to step into your next chapter.

Affirmation & Gratitude

I give thanks for renewal and empowerment, embracing authenticity, courage, and truth as I step boldly into my personal season today.

Scorpio
26 October 2026

Scorpio, introspection balances your heightened energy. The Moon encourages you to pause, reflect, and recalibrate. Emotions may feel strong, but they guide you toward clarity. Spiritual practices or journaling can ground your surge of power. Today is about integrating inner and outer strength. Growth comes when you blend self-awareness with action. Trust your inner compass—it points true.

Affirmation & Gratitude

I honor gratitude for reflection and stillness, trusting my intuition to balance strength, clarity, and renewal today.

Scorpio
27 October 2026

Scorpio, friendships and community energize your path. Networking, teamwork, or group projects may inspire new ideas. A friend's encouragement could shift your perspective. Surround yourself with uplifting company; invest your energy where it feels reciprocal. Shared vision amplifies opportunities. Today, community serves as a catalyst for your growth and expansion. Collaboration strengthens both purpose and confidence.

Affirmation & Gratitude

I am grateful for supportive friendships and collaborations, embracing shared vision that inspires creativity, growth, and opportunity today.

Scorpio
28 October 2026

Scorpio, creativity and romance flourish. Venus enhances your charm, making this a magnetic day for love, passion, and artistic expression. Passion runs deep, but lightheartedness makes it richer. Creative pursuits thrive, offering breakthroughs when you trust your inspiration. Today is about celebrating beauty unapologetically. Love and laughter heal and strengthen your spirit, reminding you joy is transformative.

Affirmation & Gratitude

I embrace gratitude for love, joy, and creativity, allowing passion and playfulness to uplift and inspire my spirit today.

Scorpio
29 October 2026

Scorpio, wellness and routines require attention. The Moon emphasizes order and discipline, asking you to refine daily habits. Avoid extremes—balance sustains energy and focus. Work feels busy, but small, consistent adjustments create lasting results. Today, ground yourself in mindful practices that support both body and mind. Transformation grows steadily through structure and self-care.

Affirmation & Gratitude

I give thanks for balance in my routines, creating habits that nurture clarity, health, and sustainable growth today.

Scorpio
30 October 2026

Scorpio, relationships are highlighted again. The Sun in your sign emphasizes authenticity in love and connection. Conversations may reveal truths, deepening intimacy or reshaping dynamics. Passion feels intense, but Saturn reminds you that stability requires patience and maturity. Single Scorpios may encounter powerful attraction, but alignment takes time. Today's message: true love thrives in honesty.

Affirmation & Gratitude

I am grateful for meaningful connections, choosing honesty, patience, and respect to nurture authentic love and trust today.

Scorpio
31 October 2026

Scorpio, career matters shine. Recognition, responsibility, or a breakthrough may spotlight your persistence. Authority figures or mentors notice your dedication, potentially opening new doors. Step forward with integrity and confidence. Today asks you to align ambition with purpose. Your influence strengthens when rooted in truth. This is a powerful day for advancement—trust your capability.

Affirmation & Gratitude

I am grateful for career opportunities, embracing authenticity, courage, and integrity to create meaningful and lasting success today.

November 2026

Scorpio
01 November 2026

Scorpio, introspection balances your fiery solar season. The Moon pulls you inward, urging reflection, rest, and emotional clarity. Sensitivity may feel heightened, but it carries wisdom. Journaling or meditation will help you integrate recent shifts. Today isn't for pushing ahead—it's for recalibration. By honoring stillness, you restore balance and create space for transformation to take root. Trust the quiet voice within.

Affirmation & Gratitude

I honor gratitude for stillness and reflection, trusting my intuition to guide clarity, peace, and renewal today.

Scorpio
02 November 2026

Scorpio, friendships and community are energized. Conversations or collaborations could spark opportunities you hadn't considered. A friend's insight may help reframe a challenge. Invest in uplifting alliances that fuel your growth. Today's cosmic reminder: shared vision multiplies success, while draining dynamics stall progress. Choose wisely where your energy flows. Connection is a catalyst for your expansion.

Affirmation & Gratitude

I am grateful for supportive friendships and shared vision, embracing collaboration that inspires creativity, growth, and opportunity today.

Scorpio
03 November 2026

Scorpio, creativity and romance flourish. Venus enhances your magnetism, making this a perfect day for love, joy, and artistic expression. Passion flows deeply, but it's laughter that creates lasting intimacy. Creative breakthroughs may come if you lean into inspiration. Fun restores balance, reminding you joy is not frivolous but essential for transformation. Celebrate love and creativity unapologetically.

Affirmation & Gratitude

I embrace gratitude for love, joy, and creativity, allowing passion and playfulness to uplift and inspire my spirit today.

Scorpio
04 November 2026

Scorpio, wellness and structure take focus. The Moon emphasizes discipline, urging you to refine habits for long-term strength. Work may feel demanding, but balance prevents burnout. Small, consistent actions—better rest, organization, or nourishment—will have lasting effects. Avoid chasing perfection; sustainable progress matters more. Today, create order that supports both clarity and resilience. Transformation builds through mindful routines.

Affirmation & Gratitude

I give thanks for balance in my routines, creating habits that nurture clarity, health, and sustainable success today.

Scorpio
05 November 2026

Scorpio, relationships are emphasized today. The Sun in your sign intensifies passion and authenticity in connections. Conversations may reveal truths that reshape dynamics. Passion feels magnetic, but Saturn insists on responsibility and respect. For singles, attraction may feel strong, but alignment takes patience. Today's cosmic message: true intimacy grows when honesty leads the way.

Affirmation & Gratitude

I am grateful for meaningful connections, choosing honesty, patience, and respect to nurture authentic, lasting relationships today.

Scorpio
06 November 2026

Scorpio, career matters are spotlighted. Recognition, responsibility, or a breakthrough may showcase your persistence and determination. Authority figures or mentors notice your commitment. Step into leadership confidently, but remain humble. Align ambition with purpose—success rooted in integrity lasts. Avoid comparing yourself with others; your journey is unique. Today is about leading authentically and with vision.

Affirmation & Gratitude

I am grateful for career opportunities, embracing authenticity, courage, and integrity to create meaningful and lasting success today.

Scorpio
07 November 2026

Scorpio, introspection calls once again. The Moon encourages solitude, reflection, and emotional release. Sensitivity may feel heavy, but it offers clarity. Quiet practices like meditation, journaling, or rest bring renewal. Today isn't about action but preparation. By honoring stillness, you reset your emotional landscape and strengthen your inner compass. Transformation begins in silence—trust it fully.

Affirmation & Gratitude

I honor gratitude for stillness and reflection, trusting my inner wisdom to bring clarity, healing, and renewal today.

Scorpio
08 November 2026

Scorpio, friendships and community highlight your day. Networking, group activities, or collaborations could spark opportunities. A friend's encouragement may inspire a new perspective. Choose supportive allies and avoid draining dynamics. Today's cosmic reminder: shared vision amplifies success. Connection strengthens your journey, and uplifting company expands your path.

Affirmation & Gratitude

I am grateful for supportive friendships and shared vision, embracing collaboration that inspires creativity, growth, and opportunity today.

Scorpio
09 November 2026

Scorpio, creativity and romance flourish. Venus amplifies your magnetism, making this a day for joy, passion, and artistic pursuits. Passion feels powerful, but laughter gives love depth. Creative projects may bring breakthroughs when you trust your instincts. Joy is transformative, not frivolous. Celebrate beauty unapologetically, and allow inspiration to guide your spirit today.

Affirmation & Gratitude

I embrace gratitude for love, joy, and creativity, allowing passion and playfulness to uplift and inspire my spirit today.

Scorpio
10 November 2026

Scorpio, wellness and daily order require focus. The Moon emphasizes routines, asking for balance between productivity and rest. Small adjustments—better rest, nourishment, or organization—lead to long-term transformation. Avoid perfectionism; progress is enough. Ground yourself in mindful habits that support your clarity and resilience. Today, steady effort creates sustainable growth.

Affirmation & Gratitude

I give thanks for balance in my routines, creating habits that nurture health, clarity, and long-term success today.

Scorpio
11 November 2026

Scorpio, relationships come into focus. The Sun in your sign emphasizes honesty, passion, and authenticity. Conversations may reveal truths, deepening intimacy or resetting boundaries. Passion runs deep, but Saturn reminds you that maturity sustains bonds. For singles, attraction may spark, but discernment is vital. Today's message: true love thrives in openness and respect.

Affirmation & Gratitude

I am grateful for meaningful connections, choosing honesty, patience, and respect to nurture authentic, lasting relationships today.

Scorpio
12 November 2026

Scorpio, career matters intensify. Recognition or responsibility could highlight your persistence. Authority figures may notice your resilience, opening doors for advancement. Step confidently into leadership, but stay humble. Align ambition with authenticity—success built on truth is lasting. Avoid comparison; your journey is uniquely powerful. Today, lead with integrity and inspire through your example.

Affirmation & Gratitude

I am grateful for career opportunities, embracing authenticity, courage, and integrity to create meaningful and lasting success today.

Scorpio
13 November 2026

Scorpio, introspection is emphasized. The Moon urges you to slow down, reflect, and release emotional weight. Sensitivity is heightened, but it's guiding you. Quiet practices like journaling, meditation, or solitude bring clarity and peace. Avoid rushing; today is about recalibration and healing. Transformation begins within, and silence helps reset your path forward.

Affirmation & Gratitude

I honor gratitude for stillness and reflection, trusting intuition to bring clarity, peace, and renewal today.

Scorpio
14 November 2026

Scorpio, friendships and alliances energize your day. Social ties may bring unexpected opportunities or inspiration. A friend's support could shift your outlook, helping you see possibilities you missed. Choose uplifting company—your growth is amplified when shared. Today's cosmic reminder: community strengthens vision and multiplies success. Invest energy where respect and inspiration thrive.

Affirmation & Gratitude

I am grateful for supportive friendships and shared vision, embracing collaboration that inspires creativity, growth, and opportunity today.

Scorpio
15 November 2026

Scorpio, creativity and romance are amplified today. Venus enhances your charm, inspiring joy, love, and self-expression. Passion flows easily, but laughter and playfulness make it meaningful. Creative breakthroughs are possible if you lean into inspiration. The cosmos reminds you that joy heals and restores balance. Celebrate beauty unapologetically—love and creativity uplift your spirit.

Affirmation & Gratitude

I embrace gratitude for love, joy, and creativity, allowing passion and playfulness to uplift and inspire my spirit today.

Scorpio
16 November 2026

Scorpio, wellness and order require your attention. The Moon emphasizes routines, urging structure and balance. Work feels demanding, but sustainability matters most. Avoid extremes—small, steady steps create lasting results. Today is about aligning your responsibilities with self-care. By grounding yourself in healthy habits, you build resilience for challenges ahead. Progress is more powerful than perfection now.

Affirmation & Gratitude

I give thanks for balance in my routines, creating habits that nurture clarity, health, and sustainable success today.

Scorpio
17 November 2026

Scorpio, relationships take focus. The Sun highlights your partnership zone, encouraging honesty, patience, and vulnerability. Passion may intensify, but Saturn reminds you that respect and responsibility sustain intimacy. Single Scorpios may feel drawn to magnetic attraction, but discernment ensures true alignment. Today's message: authenticity deepens love, while empathy builds trust. Strengthen your bonds with openness.

Affirmation & Gratitude

I am grateful for meaningful connections, choosing honesty, patience, and respect to nurture authentic, lasting love today.

Scorpio
18 November 2026

Scorpio, career matters shine. Recognition, responsibility, or an unexpected opportunity could validate your persistence. Authority figures notice your resilience and determination. Step into leadership with humility and confidence. Align ambition with authenticity—success rooted in truth endures. Today's cosmic lesson: your path is unique, and comparison serves no purpose. Lead with integrity and courage.

Affirmation & Gratitude

I am grateful for career opportunities, embracing authenticity, courage, and integrity to create meaningful and lasting success today.

Scorpio
19 November 2026

Scorpio, introspection calls again. The Moon encourages rest, reflection, and emotional release. You may feel sensitive, but this vulnerability carries wisdom. Avoid overextending yourself. Instead, allow silence and inner focus to bring healing. Journaling or meditation can help you uncover answers. Transformation often begins quietly, in moments of stillness. Trust the clarity that emerges within.

Affirmation & Gratitude

I honor gratitude for stillness and reflection, trusting intuition to bring clarity, healing, and renewal today.

Scorpio
20 November 2026

Scorpio, friendships and alliances uplift you. Group conversations or teamwork may spark inspiration and growth. A friend's advice could shift your perspective meaningfully. Choose uplifting connections; avoid draining ones. Today reminds you that collaboration strengthens your vision and expands your influence. Shared efforts bring progress that solitary striving cannot. Community amplifies your power now.

Affirmation & Gratitude

I am grateful for supportive friendships and shared vision, embracing collaboration that inspires creativity, growth, and opportunity today.

Scorpio
21 November 2026

Scorpio, creativity and joy thrive. Venus highlights love, passion, and artistic pursuits. Relationships deepen when lightheartedness balances intensity. Creative expression flows freely, offering breakthroughs if you embrace inspiration. Fun is not a distraction—it restores balance and energizes your spirit. Today, celebrate beauty, laughter, and love unapologetically. Joy is your medicine and your magnet today.

Affirmation & Gratitude

I embrace gratitude for joy, love, and creativity, allowing passion and playfulness to uplift and inspire my spirit today.

Scorpio
22 November 2026

Scorpio, wellness and daily order take focus. The Moon emphasizes structure, asking you to refine habits and routines. Productivity thrives when paired with self-care. Avoid chasing extremes—steady progress is sustainable progress. Today's energy is about aligning your responsibilities with practices that nourish your health and spirit. Transformation begins with consistent, mindful choices that ground you in strength.

Affirmation & Gratitude

I give thanks for balance in my routines, creating habits that nurture health, clarity, and long-term resilience today.

Scorpio
23 November 2026

Scorpio, relationships are highlighted. The Sun emphasizes partnerships, urging honesty, patience, and vulnerability. Conversations may reveal truths that strengthen bonds or reset boundaries. Passion feels magnetic, but Saturn reminds you that maturity is key for stability. For singles, attraction may spark, but discernment ensures alignment. Today is about deepening connections through authenticity and empathy.

Affirmation & Gratitude

I am grateful for meaningful connections, choosing honesty, patience, and respect to nurture authentic, lasting relationships today.

Scorpio
24 November 2026

Scorpio, career recognition may come today. Authority figures could notice your persistence and open new opportunities. Responsibilities may increase, but your resilience shines through. Step forward confidently, but remain humble. Align ambition with purpose—success rooted in authenticity endures. Today's cosmic message: avoid comparison and focus on your unique path. Lead with integrity, and influence follows.

Affirmation & Gratitude

I am grateful for career opportunities, embracing authenticity, courage, and integrity to create meaningful and lasting success today.

Scorpio
25 November 2026

Scorpio, introspection is emphasized. The Moon urges reflection, rest, and renewal. Emotions may feel tender, but they carry guidance for your next steps. Avoid overextending outwardly; today is best for inner work. Journaling, meditation, or solitude restores peace. Transformation often begins in silence, where clarity and healing align. Trust the quiet—it speaks truth.

Affirmation & Gratitude

I honor gratitude for stillness and reflection, trusting intuition to bring clarity, peace, and renewal today.

Scorpio
26 November 2026

Scorpio, friendships and community energize you. Conversations, collaborations, or group activities may inspire fresh ideas. A friend's encouragement could reveal a new perspective. Choose uplifting company—your energy deserves reciprocity. Today reminds you that shared vision amplifies growth and strengthens your journey. Invest in supportive alliances that expand your confidence and creativity.

Affirmation & Gratitude

I am grateful for supportive friendships and shared vision, embracing collaboration that inspires creativity, growth, and opportunity today.

Scorpio
27 November 2026

Scorpio, creativity and romance thrive. Venus amplifies your magnetism, inspiring joy, love, and artistic pursuits. Passion runs high, but laughter balances intensity. Creative projects flourish when you trust your instincts. Joy is not trivial—it is transformative, fueling balance and renewal. Today, celebrate beauty and connection unapologetically. Passion and playfulness are equally powerful forces of growth.

Affirmation & Gratitude

I embrace gratitude for love, joy, and creativity, allowing passion and playfulness to uplift and inspire my spirit today.

Scorpio
28 November 2026

Scorpio, wellness and structure return to focus. The Moon emphasizes discipline in your routines. Work may feel demanding, but small, consistent adjustments keep you grounded. Balance is key—avoid burnout by honoring rest alongside productivity. Today's lesson: sustainable progress is better than extremes. Build strength through mindful, daily choices that nurture your body, mind, and spirit.

Affirmation & Gratitude

I give thanks for balance in my routines, creating habits that nurture clarity, health, and sustainable success today.

Scorpio
29 November 2026

Scorpio, relationships take the spotlight. The Sun highlights partnerships, emphasizing honesty, patience, and balance. Conversations may bring clarity, offering chances to deepen intimacy or set firmer boundaries. Passion runs high, but Saturn reminds you that true stability requires maturity and mutual respect. Single Scorpios may encounter attraction, but time reveals alignment. Today's cosmic message: authentic love grows from openness and trust.

Affirmation & Gratitude

I am grateful for meaningful connections, choosing honesty, patience, and respect to nurture authentic, lasting love today.

Scorpio
30 November 2026

Scorpio, career matters are emphasized. Recognition or responsibilities may surface, highlighting your determination. Authority figures could acknowledge your resilience, opening pathways for advancement. Step into visibility confidently, but remain humble. The stars remind you to align ambition with purpose—success rooted in truth endures. Today asks you to embody leadership authentically, inspiring others with your persistence and integrity.

Affirmation & Gratitude

I am grateful for career opportunities, embracing authenticity, courage, and integrity to create lasting and meaningful success today.

December 2026

Scorpio
01 December 2026

Scorpio, introspection is emphasized. The Moon pulls you inward, urging reflection, rest, and renewal. Emotional sensitivity is heightened—listen closely to your inner compass. Journaling, meditation, or quiet time provides clarity. Avoid rushing into external demands. Today's lesson: transformation begins within, and silence creates the space for renewal. Trust your intuition; it reveals truths waiting to surface.

Affirmation & Gratitude

I honor gratitude for stillness and reflection, trusting intuition to bring clarity, healing, and renewal today.

Scorpio
02 December 2026

Scorpio, friendships and community energize your day. Networking, teamwork, or social conversations may bring fresh ideas or opportunities. A friend's encouragement could shift your outlook in a meaningful way. Choose uplifting company, and invest energy where it's reciprocated. Today reminds you: shared vision multiplies growth. Community is a catalyst for the next stage of your journey.

Affirmation & Gratitude

I am grateful for supportive friendships and shared vision, embracing collaboration that inspires creativity, growth, and opportunity today.

Scorpio
03 December 2026

Scorpio, creativity and romance thrive. Venus enhances your magnetism, making this a wonderful day for love, laughter, and artistic expression. Passion flows deeply, but it's joy that adds meaning. Creative projects may bring breakthroughs if you trust your inspiration. Today is about celebrating beauty, connection, and playfulness unapologetically. Fun is transformative—it heals, restores balance, and draws blessings closer.

Affirmation & Gratitude

I embrace gratitude for joy, love, and creativity, allowing passion and playfulness to uplift and inspire my spirit today.

Scorpio
04 December 2026

Scorpio, wellness and structure require attention. The Moon emphasizes daily order, urging you to refine habits for balance. Work feels heavy, but sustainability matters most. Avoid perfectionism—steady, consistent progress brings long-term transformation. Today, align your routines with practices that support clarity, resilience, and health. Transformation grows through mindful habits that create stability. Balance is your anchor today.

Affirmation & Gratitude

I give thanks for balance in my routines, creating habits that nurture clarity, health, and long-term strength today.

Scorpio
05 December 2026

Scorpio, relationships come into focus again. The Sun emphasizes partnerships, asking for patience and empathy. Conversations may reveal truths that reset dynamics or deepen trust. Passion feels magnetic, but Saturn insists on maturity alongside desire. For singles, attraction may be strong, but discernment ensures alignment. Today's cosmic reminder: authentic love flourishes when honesty and openness lead the way.

Affirmation & Gratitude

I am grateful for love and connection, choosing honesty, respect, and patience to nurture authentic, lasting relationships today.

Scorpio
06 December 2026

Scorpio, career matters gain traction. Recognition, promotion, or a significant opportunity could highlight your persistence. Authority figures notice your resilience and determination. Step into leadership confidently, but remember humility strengthens respect. Align ambition with purpose—success built on truth lasts. Today is about showing integrity in action, inspiring others by being authentic in your approach to growth and achievement.

Affirmation & Gratitude

I am grateful for career opportunities, embracing authenticity, courage, and integrity to create meaningful and lasting success today.

Scorpio
07 December 2026

Scorpio, introspection calls. The Moon emphasizes emotional reflection, urging you to pause and release built-up tension. Sensitivity is heightened, but it guides clarity. Quiet practices—journaling, meditation, or solitude—help you uncover truths hidden beneath surface concerns. Today is not for outward action but inner alignment. Growth begins when you trust silence and honor your inner voice.

Affirmation & Gratitude

I honor gratitude for stillness and reflection, trusting my intuition to bring clarity, peace, and renewal today.

Scorpio
08 December 2026

Scorpio, friendships and community uplift you. Networking or group projects may bring opportunity, while a friend's encouragement could spark new insight. Surround yourself with people who inspire and energize you. The cosmos reminds you that shared vision multiplies success. Today, lean into collaboration—your ideas expand further when supported by trusted allies who respect your depth.

Affirmation & Gratitude

I am grateful for supportive friendships and shared vision, embracing collaboration that inspires creativity, growth, and opportunity today.

Scorpio
09 December 2026

Scorpio, creativity and romance thrive today. Venus highlights your magnetism, inspiring passion, joy, and self-expression. Relationships flourish when mixed with laughter and lightness. Creative pursuits may bring breakthroughs if you embrace inspiration fully. The stars remind you that joy is transformative —it restores balance and attracts blessings. Celebrate beauty, passion, and love unapologetically today.

Affirmation & Gratitude

I embrace gratitude for joy, love, and creativity, allowing passion and playfulness to uplift and inspire my spirit today.

Scorpio
10 December 2026

Scorpio, wellness and daily order require attention. The Moon emphasizes structure, urging you to refine habits for balance. Work feels demanding, but sustainable effort matters most. Avoid overexertion—small, consistent actions bring transformation. Today is about grounding yourself in habits that support long-term health, clarity, and resilience. Balance between productivity and self-care strengthens your future foundation.

Affirmation & Gratitude

I give thanks for balance in my routines, creating habits that nurture health, clarity, and resilience today.

Scorpio
11 December 2026

Scorpio, relationships take the spotlight again. The Sun emphasizes your partnership zone, encouraging honesty, patience, and empathy. Passion is strong, but Saturn reminds you that responsibility ensures stability. For singles, attraction may feel powerful, but discernment is key. Today, authenticity deepens love, while respect builds trust. Open-hearted communication strengthens bonds and creates space for real intimacy.

Affirmation & Gratitude

I am grateful for meaningful connections, choosing honesty, patience, and respect to nurture authentic and lasting love today.

Scorpio
12 December 2026

Scorpio, career opportunities may arise again. Authority figures or mentors may recognize your persistence, opening doors to advancement. Step confidently into visibility, but remain authentic. The cosmos reminds you: leadership is most impactful when grounded in truth and humility. Success is not just achievement—it's about creating a legacy. Today, align ambition with your higher calling.

Affirmation & Gratitude

I am grateful for career growth, embracing authenticity, humility, and courage to create purposeful and lasting success today.

Scorpio
13 December 2026

Scorpio, introspection takes focus. The Moon pulls you inward, urging you to release emotional clutter and find renewal. Sensitivity may feel intense, but it is guiding you toward truth. Journaling, meditation, or quiet reflection reveals insights you've overlooked. Today is less about external action and more about realignment within. Trust your intuition—it knows the next step.

Affirmation & Gratitude

I honor gratitude for stillness and reflection, trusting my inner wisdom to bring clarity, renewal, and peace today.

Scorpio
14 December 2026

Scorpio, friendships and alliances energize your spirit. A conversation or group project may spark a breakthrough idea. A friend's encouragement could shift your perspective positively. Today's cosmic reminder: your growth is amplified through community. Choose to invest in relationships that uplift and inspire. Collaboration is your key to expansion and strength today.

Affirmation & Gratitude

I am grateful for supportive friendships and shared vision, embracing collaboration that inspires creativity, opportunity, and growth today.

Scorpio
15 December 2026

Scorpio, creativity and romance flourish. Venus enhances your magnetism, inspiring joy, love, and self-expression. Relationships deepen when lightheartedness balances intensity. Creative pursuits flow easily, bringing breakthroughs if you lean into inspiration. Today reminds you that joy is a force of healing and transformation. Celebrate beauty unapologetically, and let passion guide your actions authentically.

Affirmation & Gratitude

I embrace gratitude for joy, love, and creativity, allowing passion and playfulness to uplift and inspire my spirit today.

Scorpio
16 December 2026

Scorpio, wellness and order require attention. The Moon emphasizes discipline, urging you to refine routines that nurture both body and mind. Work may feel heavy, but balance prevents burnout. Small, steady improvements are more effective than extremes. Today's lesson: transformation grows from consistency. Align your daily life with practices that cultivate clarity, strength, and resilience.

Affirmation & Gratitude

I give thanks for balance in my routines, creating habits that nurture health, clarity, and long-term stability today.

Scorpio
17 December 2026

Scorpio, relationships are emphasized again. The Sun highlights your partnership zone, encouraging honesty, patience, and balance. Conversations may reveal deeper truths, strengthening bonds. Passion is intense, but Saturn insists on maturity alongside desire. For singles, attraction may feel magnetic, but alignment requires time. Today's reminder: true intimacy thrives when authenticity and respect guide your heart.

Affirmation & Gratitude

I am grateful for love and connection, choosing honesty, patience, and respect to nurture authentic and lasting relationships today.

Scorpio
18 December 2026

Scorpio, career momentum builds. Recognition, advancement, or new responsibility may spotlight your persistence. Authority figures may acknowledge your resilience, opening opportunities for growth. Step into visibility confidently, but remain grounded in authenticity. Align ambition with integrity—success rooted in truth lasts. Today is about leading with purpose and embodying your role with courage.

Affirmation & Gratitude

I am grateful for career opportunities, embracing authenticity, courage, and integrity to create meaningful and lasting success today.

Scorpio
19 December 2026

Scorpio, introspection calls once again. The Moon encourages quiet reflection and emotional release. Sensitivity may feel heightened, but it's pointing you toward healing. Take time for meditation, journaling, or solitude to realign. Today is less about external demands and more about restoring balance within. Trust the silence—it reveals wisdom and prepares you for renewal.

Affirmation & Gratitude

I honor gratitude for stillness and reflection, trusting intuition to bring clarity, healing, and renewal today.

Scorpio
20 December 2026

Scorpio, friendships and community inspire you today. Group projects, networking, or casual conversations could spark opportunity. A friend's encouragement may help you see things differently. Choose uplifting company and invest your energy where respect is mutual. The cosmos reminds you: collaboration strengthens your journey and multiplies your impact. Shared vision expands your horizons now.

Affirmation & Gratitude

I am grateful for supportive friendships and shared vision, embracing collaboration that inspires creativity, growth, and opportunity today.

Scorpio
21 December 2026

Scorpio, creativity and romance flourish. Venus highlights your magnetism, making this a day for joy, passion, and self-expression. Relationships deepen when laughter balances intensity. Creative pursuits may bring breakthroughs when you trust your inspiration. Today's reminder: joy is not trivial—it restores balance, heals, and attracts blessings. Celebrate beauty and connection unapologetically. Passion and play are equally important.

Affirmation & Gratitude

I embrace gratitude for love, joy, and creativity, allowing passion and playfulness to uplift and inspire my spirit today.

Scorpio
22 December 2026

Scorpio, wellness and routines take focus. The Moon emphasizes discipline, urging you to refine daily habits. Work may feel heavy, but sustainability matters more than speed. Avoid perfectionism—steady progress is enough. Today is about creating order that supports clarity, health, and resilience. Ground yourself in mindful practices that anchor your spirit and body.

Affirmation & Gratitude

I give thanks for balance in my routines, creating habits that nurture health, clarity, and long-term success today.

Scorpio
23 December 2026

Scorpio, relationships are highlighted once more. The Sun emphasizes partnerships, urging honesty, respect, and patience. Conversations may reveal truths that reset dynamics or deepen trust. Passion feels magnetic, but Saturn insists maturity sustains intimacy. For singles, attraction may spark, but discernment ensures alignment. Today is about building authentic love through openness, trust, and respect.

Affirmation & Gratitude

I am grateful for love and connection, choosing honesty, patience, and respect to nurture authentic, lasting relationships today.

Scorpio
24 December 2026

Scorpio, career matters surface again. Recognition, responsibility, or new opportunities may highlight your persistence and determination. Authority figures may notice your resilience. Step confidently into visibility, but stay grounded in humility. Align ambition with authenticity—success built on truth is lasting. Today's reminder: your leadership shines brightest when rooted in purpose and integrity.

Affirmation & Gratitude

I am grateful for career opportunities, embracing authenticity, courage, and integrity to create meaningful and lasting success today.

Scorpio
25 December 2026

Scorpio, introspection is emphasized on this reflective day. The Moon encourages rest, renewal, and gratitude. Emotional sensitivity may heighten, but it brings clarity. Spiritual practices, journaling, or meditation align you with peace. Today is about connecting inwardly, honoring both your growth and your journey. Stillness reveals truths that support healing and balance moving forward.

Affirmation & Gratitude

I honor gratitude for stillness and reflection, trusting intuition to bring clarity, healing, and peace today.

Scorpio
26 December 2026

Scorpio, friendships and social circles bring inspiration. Conversations may spark ideas or reveal opportunities. A friend's perspective could shift your outlook positively. Choose uplifting connections; invest your energy wisely. Today's cosmic message: growth expands when shared with supportive allies. Community strengthens your vision and multiplies your confidence. Surround yourself with those who value your depth.

Affirmation & Gratitude

I am grateful for supportive friendships and shared vision, embracing collaboration that inspires creativity, growth, and opportunity today.

Scorpio
27 December 2026

Scorpio, creativity and romance flourish. Venus enhances your magnetism, inspiring love, passion, and playful energy. Relationships thrive when laughter balances intensity. Creative projects flow easily—trust inspiration. Today is about celebrating beauty and self-expression unapologetically. Fun is transformative, reminding you that joy is as important as depth. Embrace love and passion with openness.

Affirmation & Gratitude

I embrace gratitude for joy, love, and creativity, allowing passion and playfulness to uplift and inspire my spirit today.

Scorpio
28 December 2026

Scorpio, wellness and structure require your attention. The Moon emphasizes order, urging you to refine habits and routines. Avoid overexertion; sustainable growth arises from steady progress. Balance productivity with nourishment and rest. Today is about creating long-term stability by grounding your energy in mindful choices. Transformation builds on consistency, not extremes.

Affirmation & Gratitude

I give thanks for balance in my routines, creating habits that nurture health, clarity, and sustainable success today.

Scorpio
29 December 2026

Scorpio, relationships take the spotlight. The Sun emphasizes partnerships, urging empathy, honesty, and respect. Conversations may reveal truths that strengthen or reset bonds. Passion feels magnetic, but Saturn reminds you that stability requires maturity. Single Scorpios may feel drawn to attraction, but clarity develops with time. Today's cosmic message: authentic intimacy thrives through openness.

Affirmation & Gratitude

I am grateful for love and connection, choosing honesty, patience, and respect to nurture authentic, lasting relationships today.

Scorpio
30 December 2026

Scorpio, career opportunities may arise. Recognition, new responsibilities, or advancement highlight your resilience and determination. Authority figures notice your persistence, offering potential growth. Step into visibility confidently, but remain humble. Align ambition with integrity—success grounded in truth lasts longest. Today is about leading with purpose, courage, and authenticity.

Affirmation & Gratitude

I am grateful for career opportunities, embracing authenticity, courage, and integrity to create meaningful and lasting success today.

Scorpio
31 December 2026

Scorpio, introspection marks the close of the year. The Moon invites reflection, rest, and gratitude for your journey. Emotions may rise, but they guide release and renewal. Journaling or meditation helps set intentions for the year ahead. Today is about honoring endings and welcoming fresh beginnings. Trust the wisdom within—it prepares you for transformation in 2027.

Affirmation & Gratitude

I honor gratitude for reflection and renewal, embracing peace, clarity, and hope as I prepare for new beginnings today.

www.ingramcontent.com/pod-product-compliance
Lightning Source LLC
Chambersburg PA
CBHW071146070526
44584CB00019B/2673